A Reading Plan with Comments

by David Enderton Johnson

How well do you know your Bible? Well enough to call it *your* Bible in all honesty?

The little book that you have in hand is a companion to my reading plan for the New Testament *(Opening the New Testament,* also published by Forward Movement). It is intended to help people—Christians, Jews and inquirers—to make their way with understanding through the most noteworthy passages of the Hebrew Scriptures and related ancient Jewish writings, that record of Israel's encounter with God which Christians often refer to as the Old Testament and its Apocrypha.

Jews who neglect to gain a familiarity with their own sacred texts are denying themselves the most significant part of the birthright that their ancestors were at such pains to preserve for them. Christians who have paid scant attention to these books of Hebrew instruction, prophecy and wisdom need to remember that Jesus insisted, "Think not that I have come to abolish the law and the prophets. . .but to fulfill them" (Matthew 5:17); his followers cannot comprehend what he meant without awareness of what the Torah contains and the prophets affirm. And persons who are heirs of other creeds and value systems will at the very least hold more securely their rightful share in the Western world generally, and American society in particular, when they gain knowledge of how the core tenets of the dominant Judeo-Christian tradition correspond to their own spiritual patrimony. For example, those whose forebears were at home in the Confucian cultures of East Asia may have been brought up to know that "the Master said: 'Make righteousness in human affairs your aim, treat all supernatural beings with respect'" (*The Analects of Confucius,* translated by Lionel Giles). Should they not also be aware that the God of Israel "hath shewed thee, O man, what is good; and what doth the Lord require of thee, but to do justly, and to love mercy, and to walk humbly with thy God?" (Micah 6:8;KJV)?

Shouldn't we all have this awareness? It was deeply moving to hear Pei Minxin, a student from Shanghai studying in the United States, insist, when addressing the City Club of Cleveland, Ohio, just as the democracy movement in China was being brutally suppressed, that life, liberty and the pursuit of happiness are gifts from God that no one has the power to deny. How many of us, who take these inalienable rights almost for granted, have troubled to discover the fact that they are endowments rooted in the Word which God spoke of old to the tribes of Israel? The founders of the American republic were thus aware: the divine injunction to "proclaim liberty throughout all the land unto all the inhabitants thereof" (Leviticus 25:10) is actually molded into the bell which hung in the tower of the hall in Philadelphia where they met.

As Thomas Jefferson once stated so well: "Almighty God hath created the mind free...the holy author of our religion, who being lord of both body and mind, yet chose not to propagate it by coercions on either, as was in his Almighty power to do, but to extend it by its influence on reason alone." The Hebrew Scriptures are where the divine intent toward a free and happy life for all creatures was earliest and most eloquently expressed, and it behooves its beneficiaries to be well versed in the stories, poems and precepts through which God's munificent will is authoritatively set forth.

The Hebrew Scriptures are unique among the sacred books of humankind in that they are holy writ for not one but two of the world's great religions, Judaism and Christianity—and are held in high esteem by yet a third, Islam. In a variety of genres—including historical narratives and chronologies, sacred songs, laws and precepts, prophetic and instructive poetry, philosophical essays, exemplary fables and cautionary anecdotes and aphorisms—these writings attest to the special and enduring relationship between a people and their God. The people have at different times in their long, complex and often tragic history been called the "seed" or offspring, of Abraham and Sarah; the children of Israel; the Hebrews; and the Jews. And YHWH (probably once pronounced "Yahweh," though observant Jews have for centuries avoided its utterance) is the personal, proprietary name of the God who repeatedly sought them out, saying:

2

"I will walk among you, and will be your God, and you shall be my people" (Leviticus 26:12).

To some of the progeny of the patriarchs and matriarchs, YHWH was principally a tribal deity, concerned first and foremost for their particular welfare; when the going got rough, such solipsistic believers were apt to be led astray. The wisest among the people understood better. They realized that "the God of Abraham, the God of Isaac and the God of Jacob" (Exodus 3:6) was "the Everlasting God" (Genesis 21:33) who made the earth and the skies and all that exists therein, who might be described variously as "God of Hosts" (that is, "God of supernatural forces") (Psalm 80:7) or "your Father, who created you" (Deuteronomy 32:6), or "the God who gave you birth"(that is, "your Mother") (Deuteronomy 32:18), but of whom all attributes and epithets are ultimately superfluous and any image is an abomination.

For YHWH is actually not a name at all, but a unique form of *hayah*, the verb "to be" in Hebrew, so that when God makes a self-revelation it is expressed in terms of "being" or "causing to be." *Ehyeh asher Ehyeh,* God declares: "I AM WHO I AM," or "I am what Being is" (Exodus 3:14). The walk that the children of Israel took with their God was circuitous, leading them through many a mile of inhospitable territory—into long servitude in Egypt, on meanderings through Sinai, to a tenuous hold on the land they were certain God had allotted them, off to captivity in Babylon, back to their ancestral home once again, and then into a global dispersion lasting nearly two thousand years. But spiritually their journey drew them onto "holy ground" (Exodus 3:5); they were privileged to penetrate the very Ground of Being.

To their everlasting credit, they inspired others to follow their lead. As the scholar Elias Bickerman has remarked, "the mission of Israel was to teach the arithmetic truth of one sole deity to the erring nations of the world." To be sure, among many peoples there was a yearning to discover just such a God as the One whom the Israelites knew for their own. As early as the third millennium B.C., centuries before Abraham's family arrived in the region, the people of Ebla, a city in northern Syria, sang to the Creator using expressions that foreshadowed those of biblical faith:

Lord of heaven and earth:
the earth was not, you created it,
the light of day was not, you created it,
the morning light you had not [yet] made exist.
Lord: effective word
Lord: prosperity
Lord: heroism
Lord: . . .
Lord: untiring
Lord: divinity
Lord: who saves
Lord: happy life.
(Giovanni Pettinato: *The Archives of Ebla*)

Later, in Egypt during the 14th century B.C., while the Israelites sojourned there, the Pharaoh Amenhotep IV—who renamed himself Akhnaton—abolished worship of his nation's many gods and instituted the cult of a single god, Aton, the giver of life, whose visible aspect was the sun:

O sole god, like whom there is no other!
Thou didst create the world according to thy desire,
Whilst thou wert alone:
All men, cattle, and wild beasts,
Whatever is on earth, going upon (its) feet,
And what is on high, flying with its wings. . .
(*Hymn to the Aton*; trans. John A. Wilson)

(This enlightened monotheism was unfortunately premature; priests of the old religion squelched it speedily.)

Nine centuries later still, when the remnants of the kingdom of Judah were released from their Babylonian exile, the sympathy that their Persian rescuers and overlords showed them may have been due in part to the fact that the Persians believed in a beneficent supreme god, Ahura Mazda, maker of the material world:

Yea, him with our better mind we seek to honor, who desiring good, shall come to us to bless in weal and sorrow. May he, Ahura Mazda, make us vigorous. . ., our flocks and men in thrift to further, from the good support and bearing of his Good Mind, itself born in us by his righteousness. (Zendavesta)

And in Greece in the 4th century B.C., the philosopher Aristotle (teacher of Alexander the Great, whose successors were to place the Jews under yet another subjugation) abandoned all pretense of belief in the traditional Greek pantheon and spoke instead of a single divinity who was First Cause of all that is:

If, then, God possesses always that happy state which is ours occasionally, this is wonderful; and if yet a better one, this is still more wonderful. And God does possess such a better state. Indeed, life itself belongs to God: for intelligent actuality is what life is, and God is that actuality. And God's self-sufficient actuality is life excellent and eternal. We maintain, accordingly, that God is a living being eternal and excellent; thus life ever continuous and eternal belongs to God: for that is what God is. (Metaphysics XII: 7:9)

Although ancient Israel's leaders sought to preserve their people from being contaminated by alien beliefs and practices, progressive rulers like Solomon and prophets of universal scope like the Isaiah school reached out to foreigners who were drawn to their God (1 Kings 8:41-43; Isaiah 45:14-24). Conversion to the Israelites' religion and absorption into their nationality was occasionally brought about by force, but as a rule it took place on an individual basis as the result of personal conviction. There were few widespread attempts to proselytize, and universal acknowledgement of YHWH's supremacy was seen as taking place only at the end of time (Zechariah 14:16-21).

Thus it became the privilege of Judaism's offshoots, Christianity and Islam, to "make disciples of all nations" (Matthew 28:19), leading others "to the house of the God of Jacob, that he may teach us his ways and we may walk in his paths" (Isaiah 2:3; Micah 4:2); meanwhile the prophecy was fulfilled that "the remnant of Jacob shall be in the midst of many peoples like dew from the Lord" (Micah 5:7), witnessing to the goodness of God and the rightness of God's ordinances through faithful observance of them. In this fashion God's voice has gone out to the ends of the earth, and the promise of God's covenant with Abraham has been proven true that "you shall be the father of a multitude of nations" (Genesis 17:4).

It is on account of this covenant fulfillment that Christianity, when adopting the Hebrew Scriptures as the first part of its own holy writ, began to refer to them as the Old Testament ("testament" is another word for "covenant"). In this context, "old" means "from earlier days" or "longstanding;" no inference of "former" or "expired" should be drawn. The major confessional traditions in the Christian church teach that God's Word cannot be broken and that the divine promise to the descendants of Abraham and Sarah remains fully operative. For example, Article VII of the Anglican communion's Articles of Religion declares that those persons "are not to be heard, which feign that the old Fathers did look only for transitory promises," and it is categorically stated that "the Old Testament is not contrary to the New."

The record of Israel's spiritual quest and temporal history is set forth in thirty-nine books which constitute the Hebrew Scriptures accepted as authoritative by normative Judaism. In Jewish editions of the Bible they are arranged as follows:

•*The Torah* (or the Pentateuch, the Five Books of Moses): Genesis, Exodus, Leviticus, Numbers, Deuteronomy;

•*The Prophets*: Joshua, Judges, 1 Samuel, 2 Samuel, 1 Kings, 2 Kings, Isaiah, Jeremiah, Ezekiel; and the Twelve Minor Prophets: Hosea, Joel, Amos, Obadiah, Jonah, Micah, Nahum, Habakkuk, Zephaniah, Haggai, Zechariah, Malachi;

•*The Writings*: Psalms, Proverbs, Job, The Song of Songs, Ruth, Lamentations, Ecclesiastes, Esther, Daniel, Ezra, Nehemiah, 1 Chronicles, 2 Chronicles.

This order, which differs in several significant ways from what obtains in Christian Bibles, is basically liturgical in design. The Torah, a compendium of accounts of Israel's earliest history as well as the precepts and statutes that enable God's people to carry out the life of service God intends, is recited in the synagogue in its entirety over the course of a year through a set of daily lections. Read with them is a series of passages from the Prophets selected to illuminate the Torah portions. And certain books of the Writings are customarily read on major Jewish holy days: The Song of Songs at Passover; Ruth on Shavuoth, the spring harvest festival also known as Pentecost; Lamentations on the Ninth of Av, the anniversary of the destruction of the Temple; Ecclesiastes at Succoth, or the Feast of Booths at the autumn harvest; and Esther on Purim, a holiday in early spring that commemorates the deliverance of the Jews from a threatened genocide during the Persian hegemony. The Psalms, which comprised the hymnody of the Temple and shrines in ancient Israel, serve a similar daily function in the synagogue, as they do in the church.

Christian Bibles arrange the books of the Hebrew Scriptures in an order which serves didactic or dogmatic purposes. The Pentateuch comes first, as in Jewish Bibles; then follow the historical books, Joshua through Kings being regarded as history, as are Ruth, Chronicles, Ezra, Nehemiah and Esther; next are set forth the wisdom books, which comprise the remaining works classed as "writings" in Jewish Bibles, with the exception of Lamentations; finally there appear the prophets, Lamentations being grouped with Jeremiah.

Many Christian Bibles also contain some dozen or more additional books or parts of books which are of Jewish origin but were not incorporated into the canon of the Hebrew Scriptures when its contents were finally determined. The Christian church availed itself of these works from translations of them into Greek made in the 3rd-1st centuries B.C. for the use of the Jewish community in Alexandria, Egypt. Some Christian communions regard them as canonical scripture, others do not; but scholars and theologians of many persuasions are aware that they provide not only "example of life and instruction of manners," as the Anglican Articles of Religion declare, but also valuable insight into the development of the religion of Israel in the period between the Old and New Testaments. These writings are generally termed "Deuterocanonical Books" or "Apocrypha."

Not included in any standard Bibles but also viewed as important to an understanding of Jewish life and belief in the centuries between the return from Babylon and the destruction of the Temple are two further groups of writings. One is a large assortment of late Jewish spiritual texts known to scholars as the "Pseudepigrapha," or writings falsely attributed to various patriarchs or sages; among them are some interesting examples of wisdom literature and records of apocalyptic visions which shed some light on messianic expectations at the time of the birth of Jesus of Nazareth. Also indicating a sense that one age was drawing to a close and another was about to begin are some of the contents of the "Dead Sea Scrolls," writings of a Jewish sect probably to be identified as the Essenes, who led a monastic existence in a retreat center in the Judean desert near the shore of the Dead Sea during the period of the 1st century B.C. to the 1st century A.D.

The reading plan on the following pages is intended to guide lay believers and inquirers through the most significant portions of the Hebrew Scriptures and adjunct texts. Major passages, and indeed whole books, are arranged into fourteen groups in a historical and thematic sequence. In the suggested arrangement, readers may trace events in the community of Israel from the establishment of the covenant with Abraham to the expectation of the Messiah in the period of Roman dominance. Historical texts provide a framework into which writings of other genres are set. For example, the Psalms are grouped according to the period in which they were composed, the event they reflect, or the liturgical function they were intended to perform. Prophetic utterances are set within records of the turning-points of history which they signal. Narratives belonging more to the realm of legend than chronicle are generally placed within the context of events in which they gained special significance. And statutes are usually set within the period in which they are thought to have been codified.

Here, in summary, is what the fourteen groups of passages in the reading plan contain:

First, three psalms serve as a prologue, giving a poetic overview of the story told in the Hebrew Scriptures.

Then, Group I describes the origins of God's people Israel.

Group II gives accounts of the Israelites' exodus from enslavement in Egypt, their encounter with God in the Sinai desert and their wanderings before reaching the Promised Land.

Group III tells of the Israelites' entry into the Land of Canaan and their conquest of the inhabitants.

Group IV details the Israelites' struggles to achieve supremacy in the land they conquered and gives extracts from the laws which served to hold the Twelve Tribes together.

Group V shows Israel reaching the height of greatness under kings David and Solomon; examples are given of the primal historiography, psalmody, legends and love poetry that enriched the lives of the people and enhanced their cohesion during this splendid era.

Group VI depicts the division of the Davidic state into two rival kingdoms. Warnings, sampled here, from some of the Israelites' ablest prophets, testify to pervasive corruption and foretell the doom of Zion unless there be a change of heart; heedless, the northern kingdom is obliterated by Assyria.

Group VII shows tardy and short-lived attempts by various kings toward building defenses against external enemies and enacting reforms to combat internal decay in the surviving southern kingdom; but as the prophets of the time indicate, these efforts prove to be too few and too late.

Group VIII relates, both from an historian's perspective and through the eyes of Jeremiah and Ezekiel, Judah's downfall and Jerusalem's destruction by the Babylonians.

Group IX is a grief-stricken composite self-portrait of the Israelite remnant during captivity in Babylon.

Group X shows stirrings of hope among the exiles as Babylonian power declines and Persia becomes dominant.

Group XI describes the return of the Judeans to Jerusalem under Persian overlordship.

Group XII gathers the poetry and instructive writings that sustained the people of Israel throughout their exile and strengthened them on their return home.

Group XIII gives examples of the ways Jews pursued wisdom and maintained loyalty to the Torah after Alexander the Great's successors superseded Persia in controlling the Holy Land.

Group XIV sets forth expectations of the Messiah in the time of the Maccabean revolt and thereafter, tracing prophecies of the advent of God's reign in the Hebrew prophets and sampling visions of the new world that was awaited by Jews in the years that led up to the destruction of the Temple by Roman legions in A.D. 70.

This plan was inspired by the table of contents of a remarkable

9

edition of the Hebrew Scriptures put together by Jörg Zink, a best-selling German theological writer and biblical scholar. The overall framework and choice of excerpts are based on Zink's work, though I have modified his arrangement and abridgements considerably so as to include all passages appointed in the lectionaries for Sundays and the Daily Office used in the Episcopal Church and other churches in North America, or when another sequence seemed more appropriate; I have also been guided by the reading recommendations in Thomas W. Mann's study, *The Book of the Torah,* and by the selections in Nicholas de Lange's anthology, *Apocrypha: Jewish Literature of the Hellenistic Age.* The captions and commentary are entirely my own effort. In the two concluding groups of passages in the reading plan I have followed the examples of Zink and de Lange in suggesting readings not only from the Apocrypha or Deuterocanonical Books but also from the Pseudepigrapha and the Dead Sea Scrolls. Several comprehensive editions of these are available in English translation. Perhaps the most convenient of these for the general reader are: *The Apocrypha and Pseudepigrapha of the Old Testament,* edited by R.H. Charles, Volume II, Pseudepigrapha (Oxford: Clarendon Press, 1913); *The Old Testament Pseudepigrapha*, edited by James H. Charlesworth (Garden City, N.Y.: Doubleday. Volume 1, 1983; Volume 2, 1985); *The Dead Sea Scrolls in English,* [edited and translated by] G. Vermes (Third Edition. London and New York: Penguin Books, 1987). In the reading plan, translations are taken from Charles and Vermes; page references are made to all these editions, as well as that of de Lange when applicable. But while these texts are interesting, they (as well as other passages set off by square brackets) may be passed by without serious loss to one's insight into the development of Jewish and Christian faith.

PROLOGUE

I Will Declare the Mysteries of Ancient Times: Psalms 77, 78, 90.
Start by reading these three psalms. "What's past is prologue," said
Shakespeare, to what is to come "in yours and my discharge." Both
in times of crisis and amid tranquility individuals and groups play
over in their minds the important moments in their history in order to
see their way through to the future. So it has been and continues to be
with the synagogue and the church. Psalms 77 and 78 are poems
recollecting the most significant events in the story which is about to
unfold, the story of how God delivers and sustains his people. Psalm
90 makes clear that this decisive intervention takes place in the whole
people of God and in each individual believer. From this psalm,
which declares God to have been "our refuge from one generation to
another" (90:1; BCP), the English poet and Nonconformist minister
Isaac Watts drew his great hymn, "Man Frail and God Eternal":

Our God, our Help in Ages past,
Our Hope for Years to come,
Our Shelter from the Stormy Blast,
And our eternal Home.

Under the Shadow of thy Throne
Thy Saints have dwelt secure;
Sufficient is thine Arm alone,
And our Defence is sure. . .

I. WAYFARING STRANGERS

Walt Disney's "true-life adventure" films used to begin with an animated sequence where a gigantic brush wielded by an invisible hand would paint upon the void the essential features of the terrain in which the live action was shortly to take place. One may similarly imagine the cosmic Artist laying down a delicate curve of green and amber tillage and pastureland, known as the Fertile Crescent, over the tawny-sanguine waste land that links the African and Eurasian continents. Across this narrow arc of territory many clans and tribes would drift, a number of them attempting to settle upon it and from its fragile ecosystem to eke out a living. Periodically their efforts would be put to nought by marauders from afar or the armies of one or another of the river-valley empires—Egypt, to the southwest; Assyria or Babylonia, to the northeast. And as if human depredations weren't enough, droughts, famines, earthquakes and sundry plagues would from time to time devastate the region. Its inhabitants attempted to make sense of the hazards and random disasters that befell them, conceiving these happenings to be earthly manifestations of rivalry and warfare among the gods.

Into the midst of this uncertainty and tumult there arrived, some time near the beginning of the second millennium B.C., a people who were progressing to a different concept of divinity. Stemming from the Aramaean region of Syria, and before that from Ur of the Chaldees in Mesopotamia (now Iraq), their first great leader was Abraham, a man of insight who inspired his kinfolk to believe in a unique God, one whose purposes were at times obscure, at other moments blazingly clear, but a God who never ceased to be at work for the good of those who believed in him and trusted him completely.

A. *A People for God's Own Possession: Deuteronomy 26:1-11, 16-19.* These lines, associated with the spring harvest in ancient Israel and the basis of the narrative read and discussed by Jews nowadays at the Passover seder, put in a nutshell the story of who the people of Israel were and are, whence they came, whither they were bound, and what God expected of them as they set about to "walk in his ways" (26:17). "The miraculous deliverance" recounted here, "through peril and in the face of impossible odds, to gifts of divine sustenance in the wilderness. . .and at last into the freedom and beatitude of the Holy Land," as the poet Anthony Hecht sees it, "represents the spiritual journey from darkness into light that we all must try to make in the course of our lives." Before this story is told at the Passover observance, Jews ask themselves, "Why is this night different from all the other nights?" The answers given include the crucial declaration that "God's promise of Redemption in ancient days sustains us now." It was in the context of the Passover, and with this narrative of miraculous deliverance keenly in mind, that Jesus of Nazareth and his followers shared their Last Supper. For the people whom God has set apart as "holy to the Lord your God" (26:19), and for all who share in their heritage of faith, the occasion when the bringing forth of the fruits of their trust in God is celebrated ought to be understood as the First Supper.

B. *The Oath God Swore to Our Father Abraham* (about 1850 B.C.): *Genesis 11:27 through 24:67.* "He's in Arthur's bosom," says the former Mistress Quickly when reporting the death of the old reprobate Sir John Falstaff in Shakespeare's *Henry V* (II:3). The audience chuckles, knowing that she ought to have said "in Abraham's bosom." Her mistake is understandable, though, for to "any christom child" in England the legendary king Arthur stood for the same kind of compassionate goodness and bedrock dependability that Abraham represents to the children of Israel. Abraham, however, is more firmly rooted in history; there is little doubt that he really existed and led a nomadic life in the Land of Canaan with his kinfolk (12:5). Arabs of Palestine, Jordan and the Hejaz are as convinced that they are progeny of Abraham through his concubine Hagar and their son Ishmael (16:15) as the people of Israel are certain that they are his descendants through Isaac, his son by his wife Sarah (21:2). Of greatest importance for the heritage of faith is the fact that Abraham was a holy man, a person of remarkable spiritual discernment and diligence (12:6-8). This quality was recognized by Melchizedek, king of Salem and priest of God Most High, who blessed him (14:18-20).

After making his presence known to Abraham over many years, God Almighty declared to him: "I will make my covenant between me and you, and will multiply you exceedingly" (17:2); circumcision—then as now, a widespread practice among the peoples of the Near East—was made the physical sign of this covenant (17:10-14). And God bestowed on Abraham and Sarah in their old age the son for whom they had longed (21:1-7). But God made use of the boy to submit Abraham's fidelity to the most stringent test, commanding him: "Take your son, your only son Isaac, whom you love, and go to the land of Moriah, and offer him there as a burnt offering" (22:2). Abraham obeyed, and went so far as to raise the knife to slay his son before God stopped him. This story is sometimes misinterpreted, especially when the ordeal of Isaac is seen as prefiguring the crucifixion of Jesus Christ. The message is not that God demands of his followers the sacrifice of what is dearest to them; it is that they be *willing* to offer him their very best.

When Abraham had thus acquiesced, God told him: "I will indeed bless you . . .and by your descendants shall all the nations of the earth bless themselves, because you have obeyed my voice" (21:17-18). Julian Morgenstern, the great American Reform Jewish scholar, draws the lesson of Abraham's example as the prototype of faithful obedience: "We may be sure that it was no easy journey upon which Abraham had to go, . . .for no apparent reason other than that God had commanded, into an unknown and strange and, not improbably, hostile world, with no intimation of how long the journey would last, what obstacles would have to be overcome, and when, if ever, and where it would end. It was a sore test of Abraham's faith in God, and of his fitness for the mission of blessing for which God had called him. And Abraham stood the test."

C. *The Struggles and Strivings of Abraham's Seed*: *Genesis 25:19 through 33:20; 35*. "Isaac," asserts the American Jewish scholar E.A. Speiser, "can scarcely be described as a memorable personality in his own right;" he "is important chiefly as a link in the patriarchal chain. Continuity is essential, but the vitality of the line will now depend on the woman who is to become Jacob's mother." Here, then, is a good place to take note of the matriarchs, of whom Genesis provides only brief but vivid glimpses. But these are sufficient to have inspired Archbishop Thomas Cranmer to urge them upon brides of his day as examples of good wifeliness. For the marriage service in the first *Book of Common Prayer* (1549) included a petition "that this woman may be loving and amiable to her husband as Rachel, wise as Rebecca, faithful and obedient as Sarah." Such may have been the qualities possessed by these extraordinary women which were valued in the age of the Tudor monarchs of England, but alert readers can discern other characteristics in them that are prized today.

Sarah was blessed with a sense of humor. She is reported to have laughed with skepticism at a mysterious guest's prediction that she would conceive and bear a son at her advanced age: "Now that I am old and worn out, can I still enjoy sex? And besides, my husband is old too" (18:12; GNB). Another woman might have been offended; she was amused. And she laughed again when Isaac was born: "God has brought me joy and laughter. Everyone who hears about it will laugh with me" (21:6; GNB); the name Isaac means "he laughs." So little is recorded about Isaac that one cannot tell whether he inherited his mother's mirth, but his wife Rebecca certainly showed herself nimble-witted and forthright. When Abraham's agent approached to sue for her betrothal to Isaac, she was no shrinking violet (24:15-28), and she used all her considerable cunning to secure for her favorite and clever son Jacob the blessing that Isaac intended to bestow on his elder twin, the easy-come-easy-go Esau (27:1-29).

Jacob had already swindled Esau out of his rights of primogeniture (25:29-34). Jacob was a smoothie, literally and figuratively (27:11), who relied on mind more than muscle (25:27). But when it came to marriage, it was Jacob's turn to be duped. He went to Mesopotamia to seek his kinsman Laban's pretty daughter Rachel and toiled seven years to win her, but on the wedding night Laban pulled the classic bait-and-switch maneuver, so Jacob had to labor an additional seven years to get the bride of his choice. Hardly, one might say, promising material to be the sire of a holy nation! But God moves in mysterious ways, and he chose to bend Jacob to his purposes. Jacob was directed to return to the land where his father dwelt. He had every reason to fear the wrath of Esau, so as he approached he dispatched emissaries to set up a meeting and arranged a lavish gift for his brother in the hope of avoiding bloodshed. He sent his wives and retinue on ahead of him and spent the night alone until "someone wrestled with him until daybreak" (32:24; NJB).

What happened here? "May we not say that it was Jacob's other self, his wicked, selfish, earthly nature with which he strove during the entire night?" asks Julian Morgenstern; ". . .and it had not prevailed; he had conquered it. With the divine voice within, the voice of God, Jacob had striven, too, and at last, after a bitter struggle, it had prevailed. He had entered upon the struggle twenty years before, a selfish, deceitful young man. Now he emerged from it. . .a new, a better man; and as symbol thereof came the new name; no longer Jacob, 'the Deceiver,' but Israel, 'the Champion of God,' who was henceforth to fight the battles of the Lord, and became a blessing unto all mankind." From a slightly different perspective, Charles Wesley, in his hymn "Wrestling Jacob," views the unknown adversary as the embodiment of Divine Love:

Through faith I see Thee face to face;
I see Thee face to face, and live:
In vain I have not wept and strove;
Thy nature, and Thy name is Love.

And what happened when Jacob at last encountered his brother Esau? It is a heartrending story, which will not be spoiled by noting that Jacob told Esau that "to see your face is like seeing the face of God" (33:10; GNB).

D. *A Band of Brothers:: Genesis 37; 39 through 50.* The story of the sibling rivalry between Joseph and ten of Jacob's other sons—and its aftermath—is one of the best-told tales in the Bible. Whoever assembled it from the various oral traditions had a real literary flair, providing recognizable psychological motivations, lifelike dialogue and breathtaking suspense. The characters leap off the page and across the millennia. The tale is utterly convincing; as the *Koran* asserts in its own account of it, "In the story of Joseph and his brothers are lessons for those who inquire" (Yusuf: 7; trans. Ahmed Ali). As with Jacob, so with his children: God picks the unlikeliest candidates to be instruments of the divine plan. All of Jacob's twelve sons are chips off the old block in one unflattering way or another. Joseph is

16

introduced as the kind of goody-goody teenage swell that any self-respecting, red-blooded, true-blue he-man would want to punch in the nose, if not worse. He is his Daddy's darling, wears only designer clothes and has dreams of grandeur beyond the stars—even Jacob, a past master of chutzpah himself, is shocked and tells the brat to shut up. Joseph's big brothers waste little time getting rid of "that dreamer" (37:19), as they call him. Their first plan is to kill him, but they decide that selling him to some passing Bedouin is a better idea. He gets brought to Egypt and sold to Potiphar, one of the pharaoh's officials. Potiphar's wife takes one look at the well-built youth and decides that he is a real dreamboat, so she tries to lure him into her bed. Each importuning is refused, so one day she tears the clothes off him, and he runs out of the house. Left holding the incriminating evidence, with all the fury of a woman scorned, she gets Joseph thrown into prison for molesting her! Though this, too, might have been the end for Joseph, it turns out that in jail his dreamy ways—or his way with dreams—become his key to success. . .

But why go on with this paraphrase when the Bible's own way of telling the story can scarcely be improved on? There are several points worth noting, though, while reading it. One is that Joseph really is an honorable, well-intentioned person throughout, even if at times infuriating in his goodness. He serves his masters devotedly and never takes advantage of them. Early on he realizes that his charisma, intelligence and foresight are gifts from God, and he is forthright in giving God credit for his remarkable achievements. Observe, too, that his brothers are not totally villainous; they have some redeeming, indeed lovable features. When famine in the Land of Canaan drives them to seek food in Egypt, and, unwittingly, they stumble into dealing with Joseph, will he see their good qualities? Will he seek revenge for what they did to him, or will he reckon that even his misfortunes were in their way a divine benefaction? Yet another thing to pay attention to is the precise words Jacob addresses to each of his sons at the end of the story when he is about to die and they are all gathered around him (ch. 49). The tale may seem all wrapped up in a tidy bundle and the only thing left to be said is "and they all lived happily ever after." But that is not how things will turn out, and Jacob's last testament gives twelve reasons why. His character sketches point accurately not only to his sons' individual deeds in the past but also to ways in which their particular descendants would either triumph or get into deep trouble in the centuries ahead.

II. ISRAEL'S ENCOUNTER WITH GOD IN THE WILDERNESS

"In wildness is the preservation of the world," declared Henry David Thoreau. To most thoughtful Americans, of whatever creed or color, the Exodus experience is fraught with meaning. Thoreau craved escape from what he called "the god that is commonly worshiped in civilized countries," an entity which "is not at all divine," he averred, "but is the overwhelming authority and respectability of mankind combined." "I long for wildness," he wrote in 1853, "where. . .the day is forever unproved, where I might have a fertile unknown for a soil about me." For Black people of his era the needed freedom was physical as well as spiritual: "Go down, Moses, way down in Egypt land. Tell old Pharaoh to let my people go." Like the Israelites before them, they were "oppressed so hard they could not stand." So had many European and Asian newcomers to America been in the lands they left; and at least for a time after reaching their new home the wretched conditions they faced were but another type of the "bread of affliction, the poor bread which our ancestors ate in the land of Egypt." And as they arrived, the earliest inhabitants of all, the American Indians, were being expelled from their ancestral territories and forced to depart on a trail of tears. Participants in the original Exodus from Egypt can scarcely have realized that the action they were led to undertake would become emblematic of all departures to seek a newer world and would serve as a sign of hope among many peoples down the ages. It was hardship that had driven Jacob and his family to look for a haven in Egypt, and it was oppression that provided the initial impulse for their withdrawal into the wasteland of Sinai. Who among them could have anticipated that in that wilderness they would come face to face with "the peace that passeth all understanding"?

A. *When Israel Came Out of Egypt* (about 1335 to 1250 B.C.): *Exodus 1 through 18.* Can a people whose destiny is to serve God and embody a blessing for all humankind shirk their calling and escape their fate? The Bible's answer is that they will attempt to do so at every turn. They will use every means at their disposal to detour from the ways of righteousness and the paths of glory, but they eventually will end up right where they did not choose to be—but where they were intended to be—because the twists and turns of escapism lead to the same destination as the direct route. That is how God's will operates in the human community. As Everett Fox, a scholar of Near Eastern and Judaic studies, states: "The people of Israel function as a collective antihero, an example of precisely how *not* to behave. They play no active role whatsoever in their own liberation, use neither brawn nor wits to survive in the wilderness, constantly grumble about wanting to return to Egypt, and at both Sinai and the threshold of the Promised Land. . .their chief form of behavior is first fear and later rebellion." What about the individual marked by God for the service of leadership? Can he or she avoid being pressed into duty? The Bible's answer is that the very avoidance becomes the tutelage for the daunting task. Here is Fox again, on Moses (whose name he gives in its actual Hebrew form): "Moshe's own journeys parallel those of the entire people later on. Like them he flees from Pharaoh into the wilderness, meets God at flaming Sinai, and has trouble accepting his task but must in the end. Here is where Moshe shines as the true leader: he epitomizes his people's experience and focuses and forges it into something new."

What about the instruments of divinely-ordered fate? Surely not all Egyptians whose crops were consumed by locusts and whose first-born sons died of the plague were personally guilty of persecuting the Israelites and preventing their departure? Egypt during the first several reigns of the Nineteenth Dynasty (1350-1205 B.C.), when the Israelite exodus is usually believed to have taken place, was by prevailing standards a spectacularly civilized society, where great strides had been made in engineering and medicine, and ethical standards were fairly high. Most cultures at the time, including the Hebraic, tolerated slavery, and the Israelites were not the only nation subjected to Egyptian domination. But Egypt's pervasive spiritual shortcoming was an obsession with death. What if the Nile were to neglect to overflow its banks next year and fail to fertilize the fields? What if one's soul were to be homeless and without sustenance in the next world? Death, in the form of increasingly severe pestilence, was the only language that God could be sure would hit home with pharaoh. The Passover liturgy, as celebrated by Reform Jews in America, draws attention to the anguish of God at the suffering borne by his creatures during the excruciating but ineluctable process of the bringing about of his will: "Our rabbis taught: When the Egyptian armies were drowning in the sea, the Heavenly Hosts broke out in songs of jubilation. God silenced them and said, 'My creatures are perishing, and you sing praises?'. . .Our rabbis taught: 'The sword comes into the world because of justice delayed and justice denied'. . .Our rabbis taught: God is urgent about justice, for upon justice the world depends. . ."

In every great religion there is a "moment of truth," a central event in its faith-history in which overwhelming danger and death are decisively confronted and the faithful are enabled to persevere, to renew themselves and to proceed into a life of awareness and dedication to the ultimate Truth. It is significant that for Judaism and for Christianity this central event is a community meal shared in the presence of God who protects and nurtures. The Feast of Unleavened Bread, like the Lord's Supper of Christians which is founded on it, is a feast of remembrance, commemorating God's mighty intervention in human history to save those who have called upon his Name; and it is equally a feast of preparedness (12:11), equipping God's people to "go in peace to love and serve the Lord." "Yet the freedom which is celebrated in the Passover festival is freedom of a special kind," notes Theodor H. Gaster, the scholar of Hebrew origins and Near Eastern cultures. "What matters is *volitional dedication*, and it is this and this alone that forms the theme of the Passover story. If Israel had gone forth out of Egypt, but not accepted the Covenant at Sinai, it would have achieved liberation—that is, mere release from bondage—but it would not have achieved *freedom*, in the Jewish sense of the term. For the only freedom, says Judaism, is the yoke of the Torah; the only true independence is the apprehension of God."

B. *The Holiest in the Height: Exodus 19:1 through 20:21; 24; 32:1 through 35:21; 39:22 through 40:38. Numbers 6:22-27.* Libraries built in the United States at the turn of the 19th and 20th centuries often were ornamented with the names of worthies whose writings graced the shelves within. Nowhere was this more startlingly the case than at the College of Wooster in Ohio. There, high on the walls in the grand entrance of the old library building are juxtaposed the names *Moses* and *Darwin*. The Presbyterian educators in charge of the college at that time thus tersely identified their educational foci: Moses had immeasurably benefited men and women by imparting the revealed truth of God's moral law; Darwin had only recently brought about significant advances in humankind's comprehension of natural law. The two codifications were incompatible only to plodding, literalistic minds. "There are two books from whence I collect my Divinity," wrote the 17th-century physician and lay theologian Sir Thomas Browne: "besides that written one of God, another of his servant Nature, that universal and public manuscript that lies expansed unto the eyes of all." In issuing the Ten Commandments to Moses (Exodus 20:1-17), God marks the link between the commandments which have to do with respect for the divine realm and those which deal with respect for the terrestrial milieu and human relationships by making explicit reference to the mighty acts of creation. Thus God emphasizes that the supreme moral law is embedded in the order of nature itself. Accordingly, the sealing of the covenant with Moses and the Israelites which is implied in the gift of God's ordinances, is performed through the offering of the blood of living creatures and is celebrated by the boon of sharing food and drink in God's presence (24:1-11).

But Moses spent so long a time on the mountain in Sinai, and his experience of theophany had so altered him in both outward appearance and inner character, that the people became restless in his absence and uncomfortable in his company. The episode of the golden calf (ch. 32) was perhaps the worst of their outbursts of rebellion but far from the last. Moses begged God to forgive the people their transgressions. God's law was restored, the covenant renewed, and a Tabernacle of the Lord's Presence was splendidly furnished, with the Ark of the Covenant the holiest object of all, to make the people constantly aware of God's unfailing guidance and protection (chs. 34-35). And God made known to Aaron and the priesthood the triple invocation that would convey God's unconditional blessing (Numbers 6:22-27).

Abraham Joshua Heschel, the outstanding American Jewish philosopher and theologian, sums up the encounter at Sinai in this way: "God is not always silent, and man is not always blind. His glory fills the world; His spirit hovers over the waters. There are moments in which, to use a Talmudic phrase, heaven and earth kiss each other; in which there is a lifting of the veil at the horizon of the known, opening a vision of what is eternal in time. Some of us have at least once experienced the momentous realness of God. Some of us have at least caught a glimpse of the beauty, peace and power that flow through the souls of those who are devoted to Him. There may come a moment like a thunder in the soul, when man is not only aided, not only guided by God's mysterious hand, but also taught how to aid, how to guide other beings. The voice of Sinai goes on for ever: 'These words the Lord spoke unto all your assembly in the mount out of the midst of the fire, of the cloud, and of the thick darkness, with a great voice that goes on forever' [Deuteronomy 5:22, according to ancient versions and interpretations]."

C. *So Near and Yet So Far: Psalm 105. Numbers 9 through 14; 20 through 24; 27:12-23. Deuteronomy 29:2-6, 10-15; 30:1 through 31:8; 32:45 through 34:12.* Psalm 105, a song of gratitude for God's "wonders and the judgments of his mouth" (v. 5; BCP) is a welcome recapitulation of the events in the journey of God's people so far, and it holds out a foretaste of what is in store for them: verses 39-44 are a precis of the episodes detailed in the passages from Numbers and Deuteronomy now under consideration.

The fiery cloud has continued to precede the Israelites; they moved when it moved, when it stood still they halted (Numbers 9:15-23). The roster of the twelve tribes as they departed from Sinai, marching behind the Ark of the Covenant, was impressive and seemed to indicate solidarity (10:11-36). But the people grew discontented, longing for the *haute cuisine* of Egypt. Moses threw up his hands. "I can't be responsible for all these people by myself; it's too much for me!" he complained (11:14; GNB). God advised Moses to select seventy leaders to share the burden of keeping the people together. He extended the gift of prophecy, with which Moses had been endowed, to these subordinates as well; their enthusiasm, short-lived though it was, shocked the prim and proper Joshua. Moses' rejoinder was that his life would be a whole lot easier if everybody had prophetic insight! Instead of prophecy, God sent the fractious people something more down-to-earth: so many luscious quail that those who had clamored for meat gorged themselves to death on them (11:4-34). Spies were chosen to explore the Land of Canaan, where they found one bunch of grapes so large and heavy that it took two of them to carry it slung from a pole across their shoulders. The land being so fertile, its occupants were gigantic and powerful; so ten of the twelve spies decided to belittle the worth of the land and exaggerate the might of its inhabitants. The Israelites agitated to return to Egypt. Caleb and Joshua, two of those who had gone spying, held out for the truth, but the people would have none of it. God grew angry enough to wipe them all out then and there. Moses begged for their survival. God relented, but condemned the Israelites to wander in the wilderness for forty years until the whole of the generation then living was dead, except for faithful Joshua and Caleb (chs. 13-14).

While serving out this sentence, the Israelites encountered and did battle with various peoples whose territories lay across the path to the Promised Land. The king of the Moabites tried to halt their progress by hiring the most potent local prophet, Balaam, to put a curse on the Israelites. When Balaam protested that he could only obey God's commands and serve the truth, the king raised the ante. Balaam was wavering when he rode off with the king's messengers. God decided to warn Balaam not to succumb to the king's attempt to suborn him, so he sent an angel to bar the way. Balaam couldn't see the divine emissary, but his donkey could. What happened next vindicates every donkey that ever balked for no apparent reason. Talk about horse sense? Its first cousin, at any rate! Those who have ears to hear, let them hear. Balaam heard, and for once—in fact, for three times—he prophesied only the truth (chs. 20-24).

Meanwhile, among the Israelites the old order was changing. Aaron died, and his son Eleazar was made High Priest in his stead, as God ordained (20:22-29). Now God commanded Moses to name Joshua as his successor and supreme leader and to lay hands on him in front of Eleazar and the whole community (27:12-23). It was then left to Moses to sum up for the people all that God had done for them (Deuteronomy 30:2-6). Chief among the gifts of God was the table of

24

his commandments. The people were free to make a choice: the direction of God's commandments was the pathway of life; the siren-song of other deities was the pathway to death. "Therefore choose life" (30:5-20). After a song extolling God's greatness and his willingness to rescue Israel, and after blessing each of the tribes by name—in positive terms that were a reversal of Jacob's parting words to his twelve sons—Moses died on Mount Nebo in Transjordan, within sight of the Promised Land (32:45-34:12).

The dynamic missionary and evangelist from the Caribbean, Philip Potter, a former general secretary of the World Council of Churches, has drawn the lesson that Israel's experience in Sinai has to teach the "pilgrim people of God" of every era, whenever its leadership is fragmented, its rank-and-file feckless and the road ahead full of pitfalls: "This wilderness experience of scrutiny and suffering is essential to the tempering and annealing process by which we gain the spiritual means to act in hope, by which we build up our faith."

III. BOUND FOR THE PROMISED LAND
(about 1220-1200 B.C.)

After the death of Moses, Joshua assumed command as leader of the Israelites, who having pitched camp on the east bank of the Jordan River were now on tenterhooks waiting to cross over into the land they were certain God had promised them. Reputed to be "flowing with milk and honey" (Exodus 3:8), it was shortly to be awash with blood. For the land was no more empty at the end of the 13th century B.C., when the Israelites first helped themselves to it, than it was at the beginning of the 20th century A.D., when the most recent return of the Jews got underway. Its cities and towns in the Jordan valley and in the highlands beyond were inhabited by Canaanites and other related or unrelated peoples, such as the Jebusites of Jerusalem and the Hivites—or Hurrians—of Gibeon. Jericho was, and is today, one of the oldest continuously inhabited places on earth. The indigenous population, almost without exception, was not about to yield the land to newcomers without a fight. On all sides, swords were at the ready.

A. *Roll, Jordan, Roll*: *Psalm 114*. This psalm recalls events in the Israelites' exodus from Egypt and entry into the Land of Canaan. Its focus on such miracles as the parting of the Red Sea and the stoppage of the Jordan River's flow reminds Israel that they could not have made the journey on their own. The psalm may originally have been composed for use at the shrine at Gilgal, commemorating the site where the Israelites had "rolled away the reproach of Egypt" (Joshua 5:9). The church sings this psalm with particular pertinence at the Eucharist of the Easter Vigil after candidates have been baptized and all participants have renewed their baptismal promises, to celebrate the fact that in the resurrection of Jesus Christ those who confess faith in him are liberated from bondage to sin and are brought into a new life of freedom as sons and daughters of the living God.

B. *I Want to Cross over into Campground*: *Joshua 1 through 6*. The deeds recounted in these chapters are the makings of saga. Exploits of cunning and subterfuge, tests of bravery, the salutary appearance of a mysterious stranger and other preternatural phenomena—such

26

elements are likely to appear in the narrative archives of all peoples who have undertaken a significant journey into new territory. The legends of the Scandinavian discovery and colonization of Iceland and Vinland, the records of the Mormon trek to Utah: these have much in common with the story told here of how the Israelites under Joshua came into the Land of Canaan. Tom Sawyer's Sunday-school teachers would have had an awful time concocting a version of these episodes sufficiently expurgated for the supposedly innocent minds of Victorian-era children. But miners in Hangtown, California, during the 1849 Gold Rush would have been thrilled if some imaginative evangelist had told them the story of how Rahab, the whore with the heart of gold, had got religion and helped Joshua's spies reconnoiter for the battle of Jericho (ch. 2). American Indian braves would have had no problem believing that the waters of the Jordan quit flowing when the Ark of the Covenant was brought across (ch. 4), and they would have understood why Joshua ordered a mass circumcision as a trial of manhood and ceremony of community solidarity before the onslaught (ch.5), had a missionary told them the tale.

People who have been forced to live with danger or at the margins have not shared the difficulty of many mainstream Americans and Europeans in comprehending the religious mindset of the ancient Israelites in their belief "that definitive actions in their history exhibited a mysterious Power who for his own reasons had acted toward them with remarkable graciousness." According to biblical archaeologist G. Ernest Wright, "the direction of movement of this Power had been against the powers of the earth on behalf of the defenseless, the slaves, the dispossessed, and for Israel this fact gave a quality of meaning to the term 'righteousness' which has become almost a classic norm in the western world. All this did not mean for Israel that the world of human events was in itself good; rather a Power was affirmed, mysterious in its origins and purposes, which could be observed within history, within all human evil and ambiguity, which nevertheless favored human good."

C. *The Heights of the Hills Are Theirs Also*: *Joshua 9 and 10; 11; 6-23; 18:1-10; 21:43-45.* Once Jericho was flattened, Joshua and the Israelites wasted no time. They set about subduing or wiping out the inhabitants of the high country. The citizens of one important town, Gibeon, managed to trick Joshua into making a peace treaty with them and thus avoided destruction (ch. 9). The Gibeonites' cleverness is evidenced by the secret tunnel and deep reservoir they had dug out of solid rock to insure their water supply when under siege; these defense works may be seen to this day. The rulers of five neighboring Amorite cities attacked Gibeon for making a deal with the Israelites. When he came to the Gibeonites' defense, Joshua deployed the only "star wars" system ever likely to succeed: he called on God to stop the motion of the sun and moon until the enemies were defeated. Once the five Amorite kings were captured and hanged, Joshua established Israelite dominance over most of the land and its inhabitants (chs. 10-18).

The American Jewish satirist Max Apple has assessed the man who oversaw these accomplishments: "The Joshua who acts so decisively to order the destruction of his enemies is hiding a Hamlet behind the figure of Achilles." In the tragic choice he confronted, Joshua "may be the first modern man. If he acts, the Manna ceases, the terrible war begins, the tribal squabbling becomes more central than the Ark of the Covenant. If he does not act, he betrays his history and the trust of Moses and God. . .Moses laid the grand framework, the idea of freedom limited by the Ten Commandments. Joshua will settle for the legalisms, the details that come after the sweeping visions."

IV. TWELVE TRIBES STRIVE TO BECOME ONE NATION UNDER GOD (12th and 11th centuries B.C.)

After the Israelites were settled in the Land of Canaan, they did what immigrants always do, they began to assimilate with the population they had moved in on, appropriating some of their customs and looking with some interest at the worship of their gods. Especially during hard times, when God seemed not to be doing what the progeny of Jacob expected, the temptation was great to transfer allegiance to some other deity who just might prove easier to manipulate. Apostasy of this sort would be a recurrent problem for Israel, as further sections of this reading plan will reveal. In the century and a half between the death of Joshua and the birth of Samuel there seem to have been repeated cycles of idolatry and return to God, with the pagan inhabitants of the land gaining the upper hand at times, and at other times God-fearing Israelites winning out—the latter thanks in large part to a series of bold and visionary leaders, including several women. These persons are known as "the Judges" because the verb which describes what they did for Israel is usually translated "to judge," in the sense of "to establish justice." Thus their role was more than juridical in the strict sense. It also embraced the tasks of divine representation and national guardianship. For they also endeavored to ensure a more perfect union among the Twelve Tribes, provide for the common defense, and secure for themselves and their posterity the blessing of liberty which they believed God had ordained for them.

A. *Singing with a Sword in My Hand*: *Psalm 68*. Scholars have found this bombastic psalm notoriously difficult to explicate, let alone make palatable to contemporary people of faith. One ingenious theory is that it is in fact a catalog of the opening stanzas of a collection of hymns celebrating God's championship of his people. But it is just as possible for it to be in essence a single song—with a few later liturgical accretions—celebrating the Israelites' defeat of their enemies in Egypt and the Land of Canaan and thus lauding God's supremacy in heaven over all the gods of the foreigners. Clearly, as Lawrence E. Toombs states, "the dominant motif is the

29

warrior God leading the holy war." The long-time enemy, Egypt, is symbolically represented by such expressions as "the wild beast of the reeds," while the current foe, the various other peoples in the Promised Land, is characterized as "a herd of wild bulls with its calves" (v. 30: BCP). Bulls were important cult animals in the worship of various male fertility gods in the eastern Mediterranean region at that time. Might not the Philistines, a sea people from the Aegean area who had occupied the coastal plain of Canaan not long before the arrival of the Israelites, have brought with them ceremonies of bull-vaulting similar to those shown in the wall-paintings of the ancient palaces on Crete? The psalm also alludes to the dove, a cult object of the female fertility goddess Astarte, whose rites may have included acts of "sacred" prostitution which the Israelites found thoroughly repugnant. Here, God appropriates for himself the image of this holy bird, "whose wings are covered with silver, whose feathers are like green gold" (v. 13; BCP), especially as an object of veneration for "the company of women" (v. 11; BCP) who prove instrumental in preserving the cohesiveness and integrity of the Israelites during the period of the Judges.

B. *Articles of Confederation: Joshua 23 and 24.* At the end of his life Joshua gathered "all Israel, the elders, leaders, judges and officers of the people" (23:2; GNB) for valedictory instruction. They were reminded that each of the Twelve Tribes had been assigned its own portion of the land they now occupied. They were enjoined to obey all the principles and statutes set out for them by Moses so that they might resist assimilating and intermarrying with the indigenous population or worshiping the local gods and indulging in their cultic practices. He spelled out rules of conduct for the Israelites to follow, and he made a covenant among the people which formalized the confederation of the Twelve Tribes. These provisions endured "as long as those leaders were left alive who had seen for themselves everything that the Lord had done for Israel" (24:31; GNB).

C. *Tough Going, Rough Justice—and Power to the People*: *Judges 2:6-23; 3 through 11; 13 through 16.* The Book of Judges contains vivid scenes of "the God of Israel giving strength and power to his people" (Psalm 68:36; BCP). The stories told in it have the ring of truth because the men and women who led the forces of Israel to hard-won triumphs against their protean enemies were anything but stereotyped heroes and heroines. As so often, God has defied conventional human wisdom and has picked unlikely people to carry out his will.

Barak, who led troops from Naphtali and Zebulun to victory over Canaanite forces commanded by Sisera, did not rise from the ranks on his own. He was handpicked for the job by Deborah, a thoroughly tough-minded prophet and judge, who rode into battle beside him. And the actual credit for doing away with Sisera went to yet another doughty woman, Jael, who brained the exhausted and fugitive general with a tent peg (chs. 4-5). Then when God singled out Gideon to lead an Israelite rebellion against the Midianites who were momentarily in the ascendancy, that secretive farmer was so flabbergasted that he twice demanded proof of the authenticity of God's call to him. God made sure that when Gideon defeated the Midianites it would be no pushover but be clearly due to a divinely inspired stratagem (chs. 6-8). The brave but unlucky Jephthah was the son of a prostitute. So as to secure a victory in his fight against the Ammonites, he made a rash vow to make a burnt offering of the first person to step out of his house to greet him when he returned home in triumph; that person turned out to be his only child, his beloved daughter (ch. 11).

Samson, of course, needs no introduction as the man of prodigious strength who brought the pillars of the temple of Dagon crashing down on his Philistine captors (chs. 13-16). But he, too, was scarcely the kind of hero that parents would urge on their sons as a role-model. Like Achilles of Trojan War fame, though for a different if equally selfish reason, he was a warrior who spent a lot of his time away from the battlefield; the scholar Robert G. Boling speaks tartly of "Samson's preference for conducting the siege in a Philistine boudoir." As a character in John Gay's *The Beggar's Opera* says, "The greatest heroes have been ruined by women." Samson was blind to their wiles long before the Philistines put his eyes out, and the author of Judges has no hesitation in saying that "it was the Lord who was leading Samson to do this" (14:4; GNB). In his verse-drama *Samson Agonistes*, the blind Puritan poet John Milton portrayed the blinded Samson as a pitiable but dignified hero; in the Book of Judges, however—as the brilliant translation in the Good News Bible makes particularly clear—Samson is shown as the hapless, happy-go-lucky protagonist of a slapstick tragedy that might have come from the pen of Eugene Ionesco or Arthur Heller. "And if I laugh at any mortal thing," wrote Lord Byron in his *Don Juan,* "'Tis that I may not weep."

D. *The Law of God Is Ideal: Statutes Operative under the Tribal League: Exodus 21 through 23. Leviticus 19.* Here is a sampling of the laws by which the Israelites governed themselves during the period of the Judges. The detailed statutes and precepts encoded in Exodus and Leviticus are presented as having been delivered to Moses in Sinai when he received the Ten Commandments or saw to the furnishing of the Tabernacle of the Lord's Presence. But a great number of these laws are specifically concerned with the conduct of life in a settled agricultural venue and would have had scant relevance to a nomadic society; so it stands to reason that they were actually promulgated when the Israelite tribes had settled in the Promised Land. No matter how divinely inspired, statutes are seldom placed on the books before the need for them occurs. Their connection with the revelation on Sinai is clear, however: for the most part, they are a practical elaboration of the principles which the Ten Commandments had established.

The first thing to note about these laws, in the context of the period and region in which they were developed, is their eminent fairness. The core principle operative in them is: "you will award life for life, eye for eye, tooth for tooth, hand for hand, foot for foot, burn for burn, wound for wound, stroke for stroke" (Exodus 21:23-25; NJB). This is known to legal scholars as the *lex talionis*, or "law of like degree": that is, the punishment fits the crime (as W.S. Gilbert's Mikado would have it), and the penalty is not to be harsher than the offense. If this principle appears cruel at first glance, look again. As recently as two centuries ago, English law caused minors to be hanged for the theft of property worth just over a shilling. Which legal system is the more humane? It is interesting to observe that while the Israelites applied the "eye for eye" principle chiefly to interpersonal relations, Jesus, in a typically startling way, extended it to one's personal moral conduct:

"if your eye should be your downfall, tear it out; it is better for you to enter into the kingdom of God with one eye than to have two eyes and be thrown into hell" (Mark 9:47; NJB).

The second thing to remark is that these laws are not only just, but merciful. The stated motivation for keeping the Sabbath holy has nothing to do with puritanical stringency or rigorous self-denial but everything to do with generosity toward others: it is "so that your slaves and the foreigners who work for you and even your animals can rest" (Exodus 23:12; GNB). In the Holiness Code of which Leviticus 19 is part, there is the additional provision: "When you reap the harvest of your land, you will not reap to the very edges of the field, nor will you gather the gleanings of the harvest; . . . You will leave them for the poor and the stranger" (Leviticus 19:9-10; NJB). It was this stipulation which enabled Naomi and Ruth to survive when they returned destitute to Bethlehem (see Ruth 2:1-2). Jesus and his disciples were enjoying the benefits of this law when they were rebuked by some Pharisees for profaning the Sabbath; Jesus invoked the true intent of both laws—and indeed the entire Holiness Code— when he replied, "The Sabbath was made for the sake of humanity, not humanity for the sake of the Sabbath" (Mark 2:27; my transla-tion). It is no accident that the second of the two commandments which Jesus regarded as the epitome of the Torah is enshrined in the Holiness Code: "you shall love your neighbor as yourself" (Leviticus 19:18; Mark 12:33). In fact, the code states the commandment twice, to make clear that it pertains not only to Israelite neighbors but also to foreigners in one's midst—"for you yourselves were once aliens in Egypt" (19:34; NJB).

Christian readers will also note in these laws provisions for some of the religious holidays, dietary restrictions, and customs concerning the wearing of the hair and beard which a number of their Jewish neighbors continue to observe. As the Articles of Religion honored in Anglican churches make clear (as do similar confessional declara-tions in other communions), Christians do not consider themselves bound by the ceremonial and ritual laws or the civil statutes of the Torah, although the moral commandments are very much in force for them as well as for Jews (Article VII: Of the Old Testament; *The Book of Common Prayer,* 1979; p. 869). But it is important for Christians to be aware that moral and ethical considerations and humane motivations underlie even those portions of the Holiness Code and other Israelite statutes that seem hardest nowadays to comprehend. Some aspects of the food regulations are intended not only to promote public health but also to prevent cruelty to animals. The law against shaving the beard or trimming the sidelocks may reflect the fact that in Egypt slaves were generally required to be completely cleanshaven while the pharaohs and their sons were privileged to wear a long lock of hair on one side of the face. Thus a God-sent liberating impulse underlies even the most restrictive parts of this legislation. "Judge not according to the appearance, but judge righteous judgment" (John 7:24; KJV).

E. *I Beg for Justice, Which Thou, Prince, Must Give*: *Psalm 82.* This psalm shows God in "the high courts of heaven"—as the medieval philosopher Peter Abelard puts it—in the process of dispensing justice. But the picture here is not the ranks of angels and archangels of later scripture and medieval Judeo-Christian lore, poised to carry out God's will instantaneously. Rather, the existential religious situation at the time of the Judges is what is depicted, and with remarkable frankness. God is supremely powerful but not unchallenged. There still exist a host of other gods to whom people offer their obeisance. These lesser deities bring about injustice in the world by unleashing forces which countervail God's will and by aiding evil-intentioned individuals who lust for power. God bids such deities to "rescue the weak and the poor" (v. 4; BCP), but the earth-shattering wickedness fomented by them and those who idolize them continues. God foretells their eventual doom. Meanwhile faithful Israelites appeal to God to arise and establish himself as sole ruler of the world.

V. THE CROWNING ACHIEVEMENT OF NATIONHOOD (1050-931 B.C.)

As the period of the Judges drew to a close, the Twelve Tribes consolidated as a nation, and Israel achieved real significance as a force to be reckoned with, both among the small states of the Levant and as a buffer between the great powers of Egypt and Mesopotamia. Under David and Solomon, Israelite hegemony reached from Mount Hermon in the north to the Negev in the south, and trade with lands as far away as the Horn of Africa brought in wealth and sophistication. But it was a "brief, shining moment" not fated to last.

A. *Samuel, Saul and the Arrival of David* (about 1050-1010 B.C.): *1 Samuel 1 through 11; 13 through 22; 24 through 26; 28:3-25; 31.* The First Book of Samuel marks a momentous shift in the governance of the Twelve Tribes. Yet again, God selects the unexpected to be his agents. Samuel, a miracle child (1:1-20) dedicated to God by his parents (1:28-2:11), was the last and greatest of the Judges (7:3-17) and the earliest of the great Prophets (ch. 3), a profession which would play a crucial role in the destiny of the Israelites over the next several centuries. Meanwhile, however, the people began to chafe under theocratic rule and wanted a king, so as to be just like their neighbors; Samuel warned them of the consequences, to no avail (8:4-22), so he searched for a suitable candidate and at God's bidding anointed Saul, offspring of a wealthy but low-ranking family in the tiny tribe of Benjamin (9:1-10:8). Saul may have looked every inch a king (9:2), but what the Israelites saw was not what they got. Saul showed himself to be no born ruler. He was by turns rash and skittish, brave in battle but inept at strategy, an easy victim of bad temper and "evil spirits"—perhaps today he would be diagnosed a schizophrenic—and irresolute and duplicitous about obeying God's commands (10:17-15:26). God rejected Saul, and Samuel was obliged to search for a replacement (15:35-16:13).

In David, the ruddy, bright-eyed, handsome stripling from Bethlehem (16:12), Samuel ushered in a real winner. If anyone in history was endowed with "the right stuff," it was he. Skill and daring, not brute force, enabled him to defeat the Philistines' champion (17:4-

35

54), and he immediately managed to conquer the hearts of almost everyone else. Saul's eldest son, Jonathan, adored David (18:1-4), and the king's daughter Michal desired him (18:20). David reciprocated Jonathan's affection and was so delighted at the prospect of marrying into the royal family that he agreed to undertake an exploit demanded by Saul as a "bride-price" that was dangerous and disgusting (18:24-27). Saul himself felt both entranced and threatened by David (ch. 19); his phobia won out, and he divided the rest of his days between combating the Philistines and attempting to destroy David. For his part, David never wavered in his devotion to Jonathan (ch. 20) and his loyalty to Saul, sparing his sovereign's life several times (chs. 24, 26). Saul's problems so overwhelmed him that he stooped to consulting a medium in a vain effort to solve them (28:3-25), and he and three of his sons, including Jonathan, met an inglorious death at the Philistines' hands (ch. 31).

B. *David's Triumphs and Tragedies* (about 1010-970 B.C.): *2 Samuel 1 through 3; 5:1-12; 6 through 19; 23:1-7. Psalm 18. 1 Kings 1:1-2:12. Psalms 89; 132.* The Second Book of Samuel might better have been entitled "The Book of David." The tale it unfolds is one of never-ending challenges. It begins in grief and ends in disarray. David became king in a way he deplored—after the slaying of his monarch and his most intimate friend. His lament for Saul and Jonathan (1:19-27) is unmatched in world literature for its poetic beauty and depth of feeling. At first, David held sway over Judah alone (2:1-11). The struggle to gain power over the rest of the Israelites was time-consuming and involved assassinations which David did not instigate and which he angrily repudiated (3:22-4:12). Once secure from internal enemies his roving eye for women got him into another sort of trouble and led him to commit his one act of out-and-out treachery: the contrived death in battle of Uriah, husband of the beautiful Bathsheba, the woman he spotted from his rooftop, enticed into his bed and later married (ch. 11). To give David his due, when upbraided for the misdeed by Nathan the prophet he had the grace to be contrite (12:1-15); and the union yielded the Israelites' second great king (12:24-25).

David had other domestic problems. Three of his sons were rotten.

One, Amnon, raped his half-sister Tamar, who was avenged by her full brother Absalom (13:1-29). Absalom, the apple of David's eye, famous for his good looks and long locks, entertained thoughts of usurpation which he soon turned into actions that nearly succeeded; David had to flee Jerusalem (chs. 15-17). David's army at length defeated Absalom's forces in the Forest of Ephraim, and Absalom was hoist by his own petard: while on muleback he got his gorgeous hair tangled in the branches of an oak, where—despite his father's plea—he was put to death (18:1-15). David's grief overwhelmed him (18:19-19:4), and he was never quite the same afterward. Even in old age his family troubles were not over: yet another son, Adonijah, became ambitious to be king, and Bathsheba had to resort to intrigue to secure the succession for her son Solomon (1 Kings 1:1-2:12). In all the turmoil, however, David found repeated occasions to seek out and honor Jonathan's sole surviving son, the crippled Mephibosheth (ch. 9; 16:1-4; 19:24-30).

Renowned as a musician and poet, David has sometimes been credited with the entire Book of Psalms, even though a number of them are ascribed in the book itself to other artists and others clearly allude to events which took place long after David's reign. Psalm 18 is certainly his composition; it appears both in the Psalter and at 2 Samuel 22:2-51, and it resonates with David's unshakeable trust in God and his unabashed self-confidence. Psalm 89 states in messianic terms the endlessness of God's fidelity to David and his descendants: "His line shall endure for ever and his throne as the sun before me" (89:36; BCP). And Psalm 132 affirms God's determination to honor David by making Zion his eternal abode "if your children keep my covenant and my testimonies" (132:13; BCP). Whether the scions of the Davidic house would indeed maintain faithfulness in Zion was to become a crucial question in the centuries ahead.

"More than with any other person, Israel is fascinated by David, deeply attracted to him, bewildered by him, occasionally embarrassed by him, but never disowning him," observes Walter Brueggemann, the Lutheran biblical scholar. "David's magnificent and mysterious person" was so multifaceted that in trying to convey his character "Israel could never get it quite right. None of the stories could quite comprehend him, let alone contain him."

C. *Solomon's Seal of Sovereignty* (about 970-931 B.C.): *1 Kings 3; 5:1 through 9:9; 9:25 through 11:43.* From these chapters in the First Book of Kings we learn what Jesus had in mind when he spoke of "Solomon in all his glory" (Matthew 6:29). Under this briiliant son of David and Bathsheba the Israelites knew stability, prosperity and peace as never before and seldom since. His statecraft was as shrewd as his shocking but effective method of finding out which woman was the mother of a disputed child (3:16-27). He built a Temple worthy of his God—intimate and exquisite (7:13-51). Note his masterpiece of a prayer at its dedication, particularly his hope that not Israel alone but all peoples would be inspired by it to know and revere God's name (8:22-53). Late in life, alas, alliances with foreign powers and liaisons with foreign women—among them the exotic queen of Sheba (10:1-13)—deflected him from his loyalty to God, to his nation's eventual doom. "Like daylight all was clear" to "great and wise Solomon," avers Jenny Diver in Bertolt Brecht and Kurt Weill's *Three Penny Opera.* That, the historian of Kings points out, is because Solomon early on understood what was *really* worth praying for (3:5-14).

D. *Royal Anthems*: *Psalms 2; 20; 21; 45; 72; 110.* Undoubtedly these psalms were composed for coronations, triumphs and other state occasions of the Davidic dynasty. Today they touch us most deeply when they speak of the ruler as champion of "the poor who cries out in distress, and the oppressed who has no helper" (72:12; BCP). Compassionate attributes like these caused New Testament writers to relate these psalms to Jesus as heir of David (compare Psalms 2:7 and 110:3 with Mark 1:11).

E. *But Little Lower than the Angels: The Earlier Account of Human Origins* (probably recorded in this period): *Genesis 2:4 through 4:16; 6:5 through 9:19; 11:1-9.* The Israelites during this era were sufficiently in control of events to take time to sort out their convictions regarding the relationship of the one eternal God to the natural order and humankind at large. These primordial legends were the outcome of their theological quest; the original audience did not necessarily understand them literally, any more than Jesus' followers supposed the Parable of the Tenants in the Vineyard (Mark 12:1-12) to be about identifiable individuals. Most scholars consider this account (2:4-25) of the creation of the first humans ("adam" is the Hebrew word for "earthling;" it was not intended as a personal name) to be the more ancient one, though placed second in Genesis by a later editor. The story of the temptation and expulsion from Eden (ch. 3) serves to explain humanity's feeling of alienation from the rest of creation. The rivalry of Cain and Abel (4:1-16) personifies the struggle between nomadic hunters and settled farmers—a conflict vivid in Israel's memory. The legend of Noah and the ark—one of many flood stories current in the cradle of western civilization— accounts for such anciently observable phenomena as the fossils of extinct creatures and the differing physical and cultural characteristics of various races and tribes (6:9-9:19). The tower of Babel (11:1-9) provides a reason for diversity of language and warns against megalomania and the use of communication skills for self-aggrandizement and ungodly goals.

F. *Songs of God's Splendor in Creation and God's Compassion toward All Creatures*: *Psalms 8; 19; 29; 33; 47; 93; 95; 96; 98; 100; 103; 111; 112; 145; 146; 147; 148; 150.* "In the Psalms," Thomas Merton writes, "we drink divine praise at its pure and stainless source, in all its primitive sincerity and perfection. We return to the youthful strength and directness with which the ancient psalmists voiced their adoration of the God of Israel." The eternal realities given narrative shape in the primal stories of Genesis are here turned into songs that faithful people continue to make their own. The question, "What is man that you should be mindful of him?" (8:5; BCP) was asked again by Shakespeare in Hamlet's "What a piece of work is a man" speech (*Hamlet*, II:2) and reiterated as a song in *Hair*, the 1960s musical. "The most beautiful thing that we can experience," according to Albert Einstein, "is the mysterious. It is the source from whence substance is given to all true art and science." And "to know that what to us is impenetrable really exists," he adds, "is at the center of true religiousness." The truth given voice in this portion of the Psalter, some of which stems from the Davidic age, "is not one to be demonstrated in the same way as is a proposition in geometry," explains the Anglican educator Charles L. Taylor. "But. . .if [the

39

Psalms] present a picture of reality that is consistent, if they invite us to lay hold on life to the full, if they offer the richest gifts that the Author of life bestows," then "as we approach God we need such a garment of praise as they provide."

G. *A Story of Solidarity and Hospitality: Ruth entire.* The Book of Ruth is a historical short story—a tale of trust rewarded, of loyalty and love transcending generational boundaries and national barriers. It involves women of courage and a man of gentle thoughtfulness; possibly its author was a woman who prized these qualities. Ruth, the young Moabite widow who braved Israelite hostility in accompanying her mother-in-law Naomi back to her home in Bethlehem, was centuries later to be grouped by Dante in his *Paradiso* with the Hebrew women who make up the brightest petals of the Heavenly Rose. Destitute, Ruth went out to scavenge barley kernels left behind by reapers in the fields belonging to Boaz, a kinsman of Naomi's late husband; she feared being jeered at for her poverty or leered at because of her sex. (John Keats, on hearing the call of a nightingale, felt that it was

> *Perhaps the self-same song that found a path*
> *Through the sad heart of Ruth, when sick for home,*
> *She stood in tears amid the alien corn. . .)*

But Boaz, mindful of God's benevolence, treated her kindly; they soon fell in love and were married, becoming ancestors of David and Jesus. A leading scholar, E.F. Campbell, Jr., who finds the story "eminently plausible" historically, dates the origins of Ruth to the Solomonic period, with "embellishments of its strong interest in right judgment and care for the unfortunates" added somewhat later.

H. *Songs of Desire and Consummation: The Song of Songs entire.* Love expressed with unblushing sensuality, is what these verses are about. Perhaps they once formed a wedding masque or playlet (the speakers include a man, a woman and a chorus) for a royal nuptial feast; more likely they are an anthology of erotic songs from several eras, the one beginning "Who is this coming up from the wilderness" dating from Solomon's time (3:6-11; REB). The conventions of love poetry and song in the Western world—"My love is like a red, red rose," and the like—are such that some of the imagery in the Song of Songs may be startling at first: "Your teeth are like a flock of shorn ewes that have come up from the washing" (4:2). But it is testimony that herds and pomegranates and cedar trees, not to mention a woman's breasts and a man's belly, are all enjoyable gifts from a generous God.

Judaism has traditionally treated the Song of Songs as an allegory expressing the relationship between God and Israel; it is read in the synagogue on the Sabbath of Passover, and the Talmud calls it "a song that belongs to the Sower of peace." In Christianity it has been understood as representing the love between Christ and his church. As such it inspired the lush mystical poetry of the Spanish monk San Juan de la Cruz, and it infused the meditations of the Anglican priest-poet Thomas Traherne: "In all love there is a love begetting, and a love begotten, and a love proceeding. . .so that in all love the Trinity is clear. . .The whole world ministers to you as the theatre of your love. It sustains you and all objects that you may continue to love them." In the present era its "I am dark and lovely" theme (1:5; REB) echoes in the work of the African-American poet Lucille Clifton.

I. *The Mouth of the Just Brings Forth Wisdom: Proverbs from the Heyday of Israelite Monarchy: Proverbs 10:1-12; 15:16-33; 17:1-20; 21:30 through 22:9; 25:15-28; 27:1-6, 10-12; 30.* Persons and peoples need guidance in order to live well. Codes of law are essential and philosophical treatises admirable, but they cannot be carried about everywhere in everyone's mind. Pithy, pungent phrases *are* portable, though, as savvy political and religious leaders have always realized.

The biblical Book of Proverbs began to be compiled in the reign of Solomon, of whom it was written that "Kings all over the world heard of his wisdom and sent people to listen to him" (1 Kings 4:34; GNB). He and the more astute of his successors, such as Hezekiah (25:1), helped themselves to wisdom wherever it was to be found. Here is a proverb whose ironic advice was appropriated centuries later by the apostle Paul: "If thine enemy be hungry, give him bread to eat; and if

41

he be thirsty, give him water to drink: For thou shalt heap coals of fire upon his head, and the Lord shall reward thee" (25:21-22, KJV; compare Romans 12:20). It clearly has a parallel in a passage found in an Egyptian wisdom text, *The Instruction of Amen-em-Opet:* "Leave [the wicked person] (in) the arms of the god; fill his belly with bread of thine, so that he may be sated and may be ashamed" (V,1; trans. John A. Wilson).

What most people nowadays mean by a "proverb" is a maxim that packs centuries of insight and experience into a few words of timely advice. The Book of Proverbs contains many such aphorisms, but the Hebrew proverb could also be a cautionary tale or an animal fable akin to those of Aesop. No matter the *format*, however, the favorite *method* of Israelite proverbial instruction was to contrast two ways of life. The right way is circumspect, straightforward and sure-footed, eschewing instant gratification in favor of more substantial satisfaction in time to come; it brings one into harmony with one's neighbor and favor in God's sight. The wrong way is shortsighted, circuitous and shiftless, enthralled in self-indulgence; it leads to isolation and oblivion. The choice ought to be obvious, but it is one's own to make, and the record of history—including Israel's—is that the wrong choice is made more often than not. For it was against the background of this Hebrew lore that Jesus taught: "Enter by the narrow gate; for the gate is wide and the way is easy, that leads to destruction, and those who enter by it are many. For the gate is narrow and the way is hard, that leads to life, and those who find it are few" (Matthew 7:13-14).

VI. A HOUSE DIVIDED AGAINST ITSELF: JUDAH AND ISRAEL SPLIT APART (926-721 B.C.)

Unity in human society is fragile, even when—as was the case with the Israelites—all members of a nation are kin to one another. The northern tribes had long resented being ruled from the south, and, absent a strong and charismatic king in Jerusalem, the Davidic kingdom was divided in two, with descendants of the house of David continuing to rule Judah (which also included the tribes of Benjamin and Simeon) in the south, while a succession of military dictators and their heirs governed the ten northern tribes, collectively known as Israel. There were constant friction and frequent warfare between the two Hebraic states, whose rulers fiddled with the balance of power between themselves and in the region at large by entering into dangerous alliances with neighboring states which never passed by an opportunity to gain strength for themselves at the expense of one or other or both. Such turmoil inevitably led to the irreversible weakening of the two little kingdoms; though, to be sure, individuals and clans found ways of exploiting the situation to amass fortunes temporarily.

The governing classes, temporal and religious, hardly exercised the intellectual and moral wisdom commended in the Book of Proverbs; they were too busy seeking status and influence. Reasons of state necessitated the toleration of cults devoted to alien deities, collectively known to the Israelites as *baalim*, but including not only the male rain and fertility god Baal and his consort Astarte (or Asherah) but others as well; their rites sometimes involved ritual copulation by votaries, which God-fearing Israelites condemned as "temple prostitution." Such cults seem to have been especially favored by powerful women in the royal households, many of whom were foreign-born, and all of whom were excluded from central participation in the worship of the Lord of Hosts. Orthodox Israelite religion was in a parlous condition, too. The Temple cultic establishment, rather than discerning and promoting the doing of God's will, sought to appease him with elaborate ceremonial, while most of the professional prophets won their bread and curried favor by telling the rulers what they wanted to hear rather than the truth.

The two centuries the divided kingdoms were in existence would have been a dismal period indeed were it not for the fact that at this time, at God's prompting, a number of remarkable, authentic prophets arose, "in all a mere handful of men," as the classical scholar Edith Hamilton has observed of them, "who had a vision of a new heaven and a new earth, a new motive power for mankind and a new road to God, and who proclaimed this strange conception with a passion and a power never surpassed in the three thousand years that stretch out between their day and ours."

A. *The Tyrant and the Technocrat, and Their Successors* (926-881): *1 Kings 12; 14:1 through 16:20*. It is not easy to second-guess historical events, especially when they took place nearly three thousand years ago and the written account of them—what Shakespeare, in a historiographic mood of his own, called the "brief abstract and record of tedious days"—is patently biased. Was the breakup of the Davidic kingdom inevitable, or could it have been forestalled by astute statecraft working in tandem with uncompromising but merciful religion? Much might have been different had Solomon's son Rehoboam possessed his father's intelligence in estimating the right combination of velvet glove and iron fist in treating his potential subjects, and had he listened to seasoned advice. Instead he heeded the young hotheads in his circle, and he contemptuously and salaciously compared his little finger not with his father's fist but with a more private part of his anatomy (12:10), a boast that soon proved as substantial as an overinflated balloon.

Jeroboam, the technocrat who contrived with the help of the prophet Ahijah to be brought back from exile in Egypt and be named king of the northern kingdom of Israel, and managed with the help of the prophet Shemaiah to ward off an attack by the crack troops of Judah, was genuinely a man of parts. He promptly acted to establish the military self-sufficiency and religious independence of the northern kingdom. He set up new shrines at Bethel and Dan, marking the two extremities of the realm; at them he erected gold statues of bulls which were probably meant to replicate the bulls that supported the "molten sea" outside Solomon's Temple in Jerusalem (see 1 Kings 7:23-25).

44

The writers of the biblical account, however, chose to interpret this move as a dangerous harking back to the idolatrous golden calf that the Israelites insisted Aaron fashion for them when despairing of Moses' return from the summit of Mount Sinai (see Exodus ch. 32); moreover, his policy of "appointing priests for the high places from the common people" rather than from the traditional and hereditary priestly caste was seen as a perilous innovation that "made the House of Jeroboam a sinful House, and caused its ruin and extinction" (13:33-34; NJB); as any preacher's kid even now can testify, the clerical insiders' club tends to find pious reasons for furthering its own interests! "Jeroboam," writes Bernhard W. Anderson in a nuanced interpretation that takes other surviving literary and archaeological evidence into consideration, "had no idea of introducing the worship of new 'gods'; rather, his intention was to renew Israel's devotion to the God of the covenant. However, his action in setting up the golden bulls was fraught with serious dangers in an environment where Canaanite religion was all too attractive."

These two initial monarchs of the divided kingdoms epitomized those who would occupy their thrones until both states were annihilated: many were as vile as Rehoboam, if not worse; few came close to attaining Jeroboam's imperfect capabilities. Confronting this situation the God of the covenant impelled a new succession of prophets to attempt to bring the people back into line with the divine intent before it was too late. As Davie Napier states: "Yahweh brought Israel into a land and an existence free and redeemed from slavery, for purposes which Israel successfully frustrated. Yahweh made a covenant in that land with David on behalf of all Israel, only to have these original covenant intentions frustrated again. Now, Yahweh's intent to salvage order from the chaos of Israel in the person of Jeroboam also comes to the same frustrated end; and prophetism, which had inspired every significant event of Israel's history, once more must declare void the movement in which faith and hope had briefly inhered."

B. *Omri and His Ominous Progeny* (881-845): *1 Kings 16:21 through 19:21; 21:1 through 22:40. 2 Kings 1:17; 2:1-15; 4:8-37; 5; 8:25-26.* The writers of the biblical record of the time of the two kingdoms cut back and forth between one and the other somewhat in the manner of a classic Hollywood western or war epic: "Meanwhile at the palace in Tirzah. . ." or "Years passed; now back in Jerusalem. . ." If the goings-on have little to do with the propagandistic purposes of the historians, a rapid montage occurs which is closed out with the refrain, "The history of (So-and so), is this not recorded in the Book of the Annals of the Kings of Israel?" (That book, which might have yielded some exciting reading, vanished without trace ages ago). Keeping track of who's in, who's out, when and where, is a chore, which was no doubt the intended effect. So why try? The career of Omri, a military strongman, as king in Israel, is dispensed with in half-a-dozen sentences, even though a Moabite stele now in the Louvre Museum in Paris declares that "he humbled Moab many years" and Assyria itself had such respect for his strategic acumen that its records referred to the northern kingdom as "the land of the house of Omri" long after his dynasty had left the scene.

It is the misdeeds of Omri's son Ahab, Ahab's Phoenician wife Jezebel, and the priests of Baal, whose worship the royal pair championed, that really stir the biblical writers' interest. The miscreants get handed their comeuppance by none other than the prototype of all Hebrew prophets, Elijah the Tishbite. Bite and bark he had in abundant supply. How he called down a drought on Israel, how he staved off famine thanks to some friendly crows and then a trusting foreign woman whose son's life he restored, how he bested the priests of Baal in a contest as to whose deity actually exists and has power—all this is told with relish. But these exploits are not the real reason that Elijah is traditionally regarded as the foremost prophet, so that it was he who was seen along with Moses when the fullness of Jesus' divine aspect, in fulfillment of the Law and the Prophets, was revealed to the inner circle of disciples (Mark 9:2-4), and it is he for whom a cup is poured out at each celebration of the Passover in expectation that he will join the feast. The reason for his pre-eminence has to do with his experience of God's true nature when he spent the night in a cave below Mount Horeb (i.e., Sinai, "God's mountain") while on the run from Ahab and Jezebel's wrath. At that time, when he felt utterly alone, he was told to go out and stand on the mountain and experience the presence of God. Then, three kinds of violent natural phenomena occurred, but surprise!—God was not in any of them, not in any of the fulminations that were so like Elijah's own endowments. God made himself known only after the occurrence of something quite unexpected (19:9-18).

As the result of this encounter, Elijah was enabled to call and consecrate Elisha as his successor in bringing God's real message to Israel, which Elisha did in a career that replicated Elijah's in many ways; and the wheels were set in motion to make sure that Ahab, who had led a mostly dog-eat-dog existence, and Jezebel, who was a bitch from first to last, died deaths of poetic justice, while Elijah was recompensed for his earthly ardor by being gyred to heaven in a chariot of fire. But it is what happened outside the cave in Sinai that is of lasting significance. Davie Napier puts it well: "the Word that comes when we emerge from the cave where alone the Word is accessible to us—the Word that comes is always the same: 'What are you doing here? Do you know what you are doing here? And, if you know why you have come, then go back to what and where and who you were.'"

C. *Jehu and His Jinxed Successors* (844-747): *2 Kings 9 through 12; 13:10-20.* A few years ago, in places like Berkeley, California, and Oberlin, Ohio, bumper stickers could be seen which read: "Excuse me, but my karma just ran over your dogma." And a conservative pundit countered: "To beat a dogma, any stigma will do." Both witticisms might apply to the next few chapters of the all-too-seldom-holy history of the divided kingdoms.

Jehu was commissioned by the representatives of authentic prophetism to mop up what was left of the male descendants of Ahab; he also availed himself of opportunities to wipe out Ahaziah, king of Judah (who had made the mistake of allying himself with Ahab's son Joram), and a party of Ahaziah's relatives. Then he made the worshipers of Baal an offer they couldn't refuse—all in all a neat ruse nicely told of, though some scribal pedant at some point spoiled the tale by giving away the ending (10:18-30; but try to skip the last sentence of v. 19). Notwithstanding all his zeal in purging Israel of agents of alien religions, the biblical historiographers had little use for him: he "did not obey with all his heart the Law of the Lord"(10:31; GNB).

So much for Jehu.

In Jerusalem in the meantime, and it was a mean time there indeed, the mother of Ahaziah, one Athaliah, daughter of Jezebel and Ahab, took advantage of her son's murder to order the elimination of the rest of Judah's royal family and seize the throne for herself. She did so out of personal ambition and also to further the religion of Baal and Asherah, to which she was as devoted as her mother had been. But another royal woman, Jehosheba, Ahaziah's half-sister, managed to hide Joash, one of Ahaziah's sons, and convey him to the safekeeping of Jehoiada, a priest of God's Temple, who had the boy crowned and proclaimed as king. The climax of this fierce struggle for the throne of Judah (ch. 11) was turned into a magniloquent drama by the 17th-century French poet and royal historian Jean Racine, with the purpose of demonstrating that even in the darkest of events could be seen the workings of "a God the same today as ever, who knows, when it so pleases him, how to make his glory shine forth, and whose people are ever present in his thoughts" (*Athaliah,* I:1).

God's mindfulness of the best interests of Judah was recompensed in how the winner in the struggle dealt with the need for repairs to the Temple and the necessity of preserving the kingdom from the onslaught of the king of Syria, though the latter transaction proved fatal (ch. 12). And now, back in the north. . .A change of heir, but not a change in the royal ways, alas. On his deathbed, Elisha the prophet tried to teach king Jehoash how to act to defend *his* kingdom against the Syrians, but to little avail.

D. *A Farmer Who Wouldn't Use Fancy Words: 2 Kings 14. Amos 1 through 8.*

Amaziah II, the son of Joash, king of Judah, was an intemperate man, like his ancestor Rehoboam. After avenging his father's murder, he made war on Edom, at his southeastern flank, with considerable success. This made him attempt to establish his equality vis-a-vis Israel. The current king of that realm, Jehoash, Jehu's grandson, replied with an insulting parable (2 Kings 14:9-10), but Amaziah II refused to get the message. The two thereupon met in battle inside the territory of Judah, Amaziah II was defeated, the walls of Jerusalem were demolished, and the Temple was stripped of its precious ornaments. Astonishingly, Amaziah II outlived Jehoash by

15 years, but he was so ineffectual that he was conspired against and was assassinated. His young son Azariah, better known as Uzziah, was placed on the throne of Judah; he prudently avoided contention with Israel but instead reached south, recovering and restoring the port of Elath on the Red Sea. More about him later. Meanwhile in Israel, Jeroboam II, son of Jehoash, gained the throne; he, too, consolidated his reign, confirming Israel's hold on the Jordan valley and extending his northern border to Hamath in Syria. So, all was well with the two kingdoms? No.

Though there was the outward appearance of peace and prosperity, the inner life of the two Hebraic states was a mess. Things were way out of line and needed truing up. So said Amos, a man of Tekoa in Judah, whom God sent to Israel to deliver the divine judgment concerning the condition of things. Amos, to be sure, was thoroughly ecumenical in his prophecies of doom: things were rotten in Syria, Philistia, Tyre, Edom, Ammon, Moab and Judah, but they were rottenest in the state of Israel (Amos 1:3-3:2). Just who was this fellow Amos to carry on in this way? demanded one of Jeroboam II's hireling priests. "I am a herdsman, and I take care of fig trees. But the Lord took me from my work as a shepherd and ordered me to come and prophesy to his people Israel. So now listen to what the Lord says" (7:14-16; GNB).

Amos was the first of the great prophets of Israel whose utterances have been preserved substantially intact. His words have the plain-spoken directness familiar to Americans in the poetry of Robert Frost or the fiction of John Steinbeck. His language is graphic, and his symbolism down-to-earth. Like many truthtellers in the Hebrew tongue, Amos often resorted to puns to get his point across. A minor change of produce in 8:1-3 will demonstrate the effectiveness of this device: "In another vision I saw a basket full of squashes. The Lord asked, 'Amos, what do you see?' 'A basket of squashes,' I replied. The Lord said to me, 'The time has come for my people Israel to be squashed to a pulp. . .'"

Amos' language was caked with soil, but his insights and purposes were far from mundane: "Seek him who made the Pleiades and Orion, and turns deep darkness into the morning, and darkens the day into the night; who calls for the waters of the sea and pours them out upon the surface of the earth: The Lord is his name" (5:8; BCP, after RSV).

As Edith Hamilton has so rightly said, the "new vision" to be found in Amos and his immediate successors "of what God required brought with it a new vision of what God Himself was, in Whose presence was no place for trivialities. From spectacle and show He was completely aloof, from colorful trappings and sonorous formulas and elaborated intricacies of movement and all the rest that made up the drama of worship, so dear to human performers and spectators. He wanted one thing only, men of good will. To worship God was to do what God commanded, and His commandment was to bring about justice and mercy, just precisely this and nothing else. His worship had no connection with men's actions toward each other. There was no conceivable form of worship which could bring men into relation with Him. The only way to find Him was to do his will."

E. *A Gentle Man Who Went Muckraking*: *Hosea 1 and 2.* Amos told off the supercilious priest of Bethel by announcing that the priest's wife would one day be selling herself on the street corner. Well, Amos was a clodhopper—what else could you expect from that sort? And he was from below the border—you know how crude they can be down south. So God in his mercy inspired Hosea, a fastidious and kindly northerner, to wed a slut in order to bring even closer to home the message that the kingdom of Israel had become a whoredom whose red light was about to be snuffed out. To the children born to this marriage with Gomer, the paternity of whom Hosea could never be sure of, he gave the painful but telling names of Jezreel ("God sows," a pleasant-sounding concept, did the name not in fact refer to the grisly massacre that Jehu carried out at the town of that name; see 2 Kings 10:7-11), Loruhamah ("unloved") and Loammi ("no folk of mine"); for English names of similar shock value, try "Kent" (as in "Kent State massacre"), "Gillyvor" (Shakespeare's word for "wall-flower") and "Perdita" ("abandoned"). The message is plain: unless Israel wipes the paint from her face and mends her ways, God will strip her naked and show her children no pity.

But neither God nor Hosea could bear not to hold out the offer of reconciliation and ultimate reunion, if only Israel would repent. "In order to bring acutely home to Israel this faithlessness," writes the novelist Mary Ellen Chase, "Hosea often uses the term *knowledge* of God. The word clearly means to him not only knowledge in the common conception of intelligent understanding, but also in its Old Testament meaning of intimacy. He even extends its meaning to include that intimacy by which repeatedly in Old Testament story a man *knows* a woman in the marital sense. To Hosea to *know* God is not merely a matter of right thinking or even of right worship. It is rather a matter of tender and intimate communion with Him which must result, as in human devotion at its best, in steadfast love and faithfulness."

F. *Disease in Judah, Doomsday in Israel* (747-722): *2 Kings 15:1 through 16:5. Isaiah 7:1-9. 2 Kings 16:7 through 17:41.* Though it was Israel that was mortally ill, it was on Uzziah, king of Judah, that the physical symptoms of sickness showed up. This was ironic in the extreme, because by prevailing standards Uzziah was a good king who mostly "did what was pleasing to the Lord" (2 Kings 15:3; GNB). Uzziah contracted leprosy and had to live in a house off by itself, while his son Jotham acted as regent (15:5). Hansen's disease, as leprosy is now called, evoked in biblical times the same dread that AIDS does nowadays; and, much as some irrational or judgmental persons currently believe about the victims of AIDS, those who fell prey to its outward and visible ravages were often regarded as having an inner and spiritual malady as well. Hence the significance of Uzziah when his name crops up in accounts of the careers of prophets of his era.

But if Judah was a sanatorium, Israel was a morgue. Thugs knifed their way to the throne in swift succession. One of the bloodiest was Menachem (a name that still has a menacing sound), who wreaked vengeance on a place called Tappuah because it would not surrender to him, ripping open the wombs of all its pregnant women (2 Kings 15:17); later, finding it needful to bribe King Tiglath-Pileser III of Assyria not to invade Israel, he performed similar radical surgery on the moneybags of the country's wealthiest men. So things went, getting ever worse, in Israel.

And in Judah, Uzziah's grandson Ahaz succeeded his father Jotham as king and was an utter disgrace to his parentage; under attack from

51

Israel and Syria, he tried to gain favor with the celestial powers by sacrificing his own son as a burnt offering (16:3), and when that didn't work he purchased a temporary alliance with Tiglath-Pileser which enabled him to defeat his immediate enemies. God, through the agency of Isaiah, the latest authentic prophet to emerge, tried fruitlessly to warn Ahaz not to get carried away in trying to stave off Israel and Syria, for they would soon be burnt-out cases (Isaiah 7:1-9). But Ahaz, when he met Tiglath-Pileser in Damascus on a state visit, acted like a hick on his first visit to the big town, who couldn't wait to try out back home all the fancy new ways he discovered abroad; which only succeeded in impressing the Assyrians with what an uncouth weakling he was.

The two kingdoms might have limped on in this fashion for some time longer had not the latest king of Israel, Hoshea, decided one year to stop payment of the tribute money to Shalmaneser, Tiglath-Pileser's successor, which by then had become an extortionate annual event. Instead, he appealed to Egypt for help. This was a fatal mistake. Shalmaneser invaded the northern kingdom, conquered Samaria, its capital, after a long siege, carted most of the people away to exile in Mesopotamia, where they at length were absorbed into the local population, and resettled the land with people from elsewhere. Israel thus ceased to exist. Judah survived its kindred kingdom by little more that a century.

G. *Hosea on His Nation's Debilitating Diseases: Hosea 4:1 through 7:2; 8; 10:1 through 11:11; 13:4 through 14:9.* As he watched his nation sink into irreversible decline, Hosea continued to inveigh against its leadership and warn its people, using language that compared Israel's condition (and Judah's, too) to ailments brought on through promiscuous liaisons and reckless, rakish behavior: "I shall be like ringworm for Ephraim and like gangrene for the House of Judah" (5:12; NJB). Other images smack of blighted husbandry: "so-called justice spreads like a poisonous weed along the furrows of the fields" (10:4; NJB). In a heartrending plea, Hosea concluded by begging the people of Israel to "return to the Lord your God." He conveyed God's offer: "I will be to the people of Israel like rain in a dry land. They will blossom like flowers; they will be firmly rooted like

52

the trees of Lebanon. They will be alive with new growth. . ." (14:1, 5-6; GNB). But the expiring whore was too stricken to respond, and the "new growth" would spring from a collateral branch. "The waywardness of Israel," to the American Jewish novelist and journalist James Atlas, serves as "a parable of human arrogance. It's not only our sins—whoring, greed, adultery—that condemn us, it's what they represent: a putting of our desires before those of God."

H. *Until the Land Is Desolate: Isaiah 6; 1:21 through 5:30; 7:10 through 10:4.* Much as Hosea was impelled to plead with the aberrant people in the northern kingdom to return to their yearning God, Isaiah was called to bring God's message of disappointed love to the people in the south. Isaiah may well have been a priest, for the call came to him while he was assisting at the liturgy in the Temple on Mount Zion. Just as the choir of priests was about to intone the "Holy, holy, holy," one of the great statues of winged seraphim which stood guard over the Ark of the Covenant ceased to be an artifact and became one of the heavenly powers waiting on the Almighty, whose presence filled the Temple. The song of sanctification became the music of the spheres, the very rhythm of the universe itself. And Isaiah felt utterly desolate. He already knew that he dwelt among an unclean people: his dying king's disease proved that. But he, too, was filthy; his lips were unclean for having had the temerity to sing of God's holiness when before the face of God himself, rather the way rabbis were later to consider that touching the divine Word of Scripture defiled the hands. But the great seraph took a coal from the altar of burnt offerings and purged Isaiah's lips with it, much as a cave where lepers dwelt would be burned out with fire to cleanse it of the pestilence. And Isaiah accepted God's commission to speak in his behalf.

But if Isaiah felt lost before, he felt devastated now, for he was told to convey to his people a message that they were not to believe, and so bring destruction on themselves. What an excruciating task! Yet Isaiah faithfully carried it out, speaking his piece in some of the most sublime religious poetry ever composed. As to its content, Isaiah's earliest pronouncements were made in figures similar to those of Hosea: "How has she turned adulteress, the faithful city, so upright!" (1:21; NAB). He issued a set of reproaches like those of Amos (5:8-

23; 10:1-4), except that his had to do with internal misdeeds in Judah itself. But he also combined images that were all about him in ways uniquely his own: God's lovesong in his vineyard that turns into a dirge as the cultivated vines are supplanted by wild stock (5:1-7); the war song full of fire and trampling boots into the midst of which suddenly bursts the prediction of a child to be born, whose name will be called "Wonderful Counselor, Mighty God, Everlasting Father, Prince of Peace" (ch. 9). Isaiah would continue to be heard from, but seldom heeded, for nearly a quarter of a century. "The basic theme of Isaiah's teaching is that it is God and not man, who determines history, whatever appearances may suggest," J.B. Phillips has written. "Clever political moves and alliances may appear advantageous, but they are useless and indeed evil if they lead the nation away from its trust in God."

I. *Zion, City of Our God: Psalms 24; 15; 46; 48; 65; 84; 122; 134.* Of cities esteemed for their holiness, Jerusalem "the golden" lacks the awesome natural setting of pagan Delphi in Greece, where, already in the 8th century B.C., "shrines were bursting with feast-day offerings, streets were bustling with welcome of far-off friends," as the poet Bacchylides would one day describe it. Nor have its monuments ever quite dazzled the eye as once did those of Athens at its acme, "glistening, violet-wreathed and worthy of song, citadel of the divine," if Pindar's words do not exaggerate. At various times in Jerusalem's history—including the present day—it has been possible to "make the circuit of Zion; walk round about her; count the number of her towers" (48:11; BCP); but reliance on her manmade bulwarks has always proved foolhardy. God alone is his people's "refuge and strength" (46:1; BCP), and the city of God's abode has beauty only to the extent that its human inhabitants "have clean hands and a pure heart" (24:4; BCP). It is in pursuit of these spiritual qualities that people's "hearts are set on the pilgrims' way" that leads to Mount Zion (84:4; BCP), and their souls have time and again been "glad when they said to me, 'Let us go to the house of the Lord'" (122:1; BCP). Regrettably, Jerusalem has seldom, if ever, been at one with itself, nor has quietness prevailed within its towers. Still, the ideal state of being envisioned in this group of psalms has always been aspired to by God's people, and these were the songs of Zion that the remnant of Judah would find themselves unable to sing when held captive in Babylon.

VII. THE DOGS OF WAR: JUDAH AFTER ISRAEL'S DOWNFALL (724-608 B.C.)

Like ravening wolves. . .Prophets, poets and other farsighted persons have again and again used canine imagery to represent the forces of strife and rapine between and within human communities. "Let slip the dogs of war!" cries Mark Antony in Shakespeare's *Julius Caesar* as he meditates on revenge against his mentor's killers. Perhaps the most vivid such use is one of the earliest, in the *Iliad,* which Homer was putting into final shape not long before Assyrian troops laid siege to Hezekiah's Jerusalem. Here is an elite corps of soldiers in mid-attack:

> *Like ravening wolves,*
> *Terribly strong, that, having slain among*
> *The hills an antlered stag of mighty size,*
> *Tear and devour it, while their jaws are stained*
> *With its red blood, then gather in a herd*
> *About some darkly flowing stream, and lap*
> *The sullen water with their slender tongues,*
> *And drop the clots of blood from their grim mouths,*
> *And, although gorged, are fierce and fearless still,—*
> *(Iliad, XVI: 156-163;* trans. William Cullen Bryant)

For residents of Jerusalem and other fortified towns of Judah after the downfall of Israel who were perceptive enough to realize that their own doom was not far off, the wait must have been agonizing. To know that, even if not circling below the city walls, the predators were just over the horizon. . .

A. *A Sagacious Quarry and His Stupid Whelps* (724-640): *2 Kings 18 through 21.* Judah might swiftly have suffered the same fate as its sister kingdom to the north were it not for the fact that its king at the time was a remarkable man, Hezekiah. "Judah never had another king like him, either before or after his time. He was faithful to the Lord and never disobeyed him. . .So the Lord was with him, and he was successful in everything he did" (18:5-7; GNB). Politically, he prudently maintained his little realm's quasi-independence by keeping up the tributary payments to Assyria that his father Ahaz had started; he continued them as long as Shalmaneser and his successor Sargon reigned in Nineveh. With Sargon's death and the accession of Sennacherib to the Assyrian throne, Hezekiah sensed that the Mesopotamian superpower might not be as omnipotent as it appeared. He led a revolt of the small vassal states in the Levant, most of which immediately capitulated when "the Assyrian came down like the wolf on the fold," to quote Lord Byron's memorable phrase. Sennacherib overran most of Judah's cities and towns, but Hezekiah, who had carefully ensured his capital's water supply by drilling a tunnel to the city's main spring (a masterpiece of engineering that can be seen to this day), was able to hold out in Jerusalem. Sennacherib's own official account of this campaign is extant:

As to Hezekiah, the Jew, he did not submit to my yoke, I laid seige to 46 of his strong cities, walled forts and to the countless small villages in their vicinity. . .I drove out (of them) 200, 150 people, young and old, male and female, horses, mules, donkeys, camels, big and small cattle beyond counting, and considered (them) booty. Himself I made a prisoner in Jerusalem, his royal residence, like a bird in a cage. I surrounded him with earthwork in order to molest those who were leaving his city's gate. (Prism of Sennacherib; trans. A. Leo Oppenheim)

The Assyrian record, preserved on a clay prism, and the biblical narrative corroborate one another in a number of important details. They both witness to Sennacherib's boastfulness: Sennacherib himself speaks of "the terror-inspiring splendor of my lordship," and in 2 Kings, his cupbearer-in-chief insults Hezekiah as "no match for even the lowest ranking Assyrian official" (18:24; GNB). Both narratives agree that Hezekiah handed over a huge indemnity, though the Bible states that it was paid *before* the siege of Jerusalem in a vain effort to make the Assyrian tyrant go away, while Sennacherib states that the tribute was sent to him in Nineveh *after* he returned to his capital. And it is evident from both accounts that Sennacherib departed without dislodging Hezekiah or displacing the whole population of Judah, but

Sennacherib is utterly silent as to the reason for his departure, while the writer of Kings does not hesitate to say why (19:32-36); braggarts usually *do* button up about their failures, and diseases like typhoid and cholera have been known to wipe out armies more or less overnight. What's more, both Hezekiah and his spiritual advisor, Isaiah, could discern the signs of the times: they could tell that Assyria was ripe for a palace revolution (19:37), and that Nineveh's day was coming to a close and Babylon's was again in the ascendant, even though there already were indications that that would prove a dubious blessing for Judah (20:12-19).

A seasoned soldier-poet, Archilochus of Paros in the Greek islands, who was roughly Hezekiah's contemporary, wrote that "the fox knows many things, the hedgehog one—but a big one." For the author of Kings, the one thing needful that Hezekiah knew was to trust God totally; this saved his kingdom when under attack and his health when near death. Unfortunately for Judah, his son and grandson did not follow his example; they reverted to type, royal Israelite style, and hedged their religious bets, with Manasseh even taking up the astrological practices fashionable in Babylon.

B. *A Husbandman Who Howled like a Jackal: Micah 1 through 3; 5:10 through 7:20.* Micah, like Amos, came from the countryside, but his was lush tillage and pastureland, not the hardscrabble margin of Tekoa, so it was in bitter irony that he declared that he would howl like a jackal and mourn like a creature of the desert (1:8). Micah was certain that the fate which overtook Samaria was soon to descend upon Judah, and he uncannily named all the cities and towns of the coastal plain and piedmont that Sennacherib was shortly to overrun (1:10-15). Possessing all the ingrained principles of an honest farmer, he was aghast at the loose living, the dabbling in witchcraft, the cheating, the betrayal of family and neighbor that he saw in Jerusalem; for the cityfolk of Judah were really making a bundle as the Liechtenstein or Hong Kong of their day, the necessary free-trade zone where Egypt and Mesopotamia—enemies from time immemorial—could make under-the-table deals with each other. "The sort of prophet this people wants is a windbag and a liar, prophesying a future of 'wines and spirits'" (2:11; trans. J.B. Phillips). Even those smart enough to know that there would be a morning-after reckoned that they could buy God off with a hefty donation, sacrificing their own children as a last resort (6:7). This kind of pseudo-religious selfishness draws forth from Micah one of the greatest theological statements in the Hebrew Scriptures: God "has showed you, O man, what is good; and what does the Lord require of you but to do justice, and to love kindness, and to walk humbly with your God?" (6:8; the Hebrew words are kaleidoscopic with many more shades of meaning than any one set of English equivalents can possibly reflect: with equal accuracy the NEB translates this as "to act justly, to love loyalty, to walk wisely before your God"). As the Anglican lay theologian Marianne Micks has noted, the prophet "was not giving humanity generalized truths about the nature of pure religion. He was lashing out against the apostasy of a people who had substituted external religious forms for close covenant relationship with the Lord, the source of their being."

Because of Judah's solipsism and religious superficiality, Micah the humble husbandman in God's acreage foresaw the day when "Zion shall be plowed as a field, Jerusalem shall become a heap of ruins" (3:12). In the distant future, the Holy City would have its inhabitants restored to it, and their enemies' "land shall be a waste because of its citizens, as a result of their deeds" (7:13; NAB), though this will come about thanks to God's solicitude and not owing to any virtue in his people: "Who is there like you, the God who removes guilt and pardons sin for the remnant of his inheritance; Who does not persist in anger forever, but delights rather in clemency?" (7:18; NAB).

C. *The Hut in the Vineyard that Floods Will Overwhelm: Isaiah 1:1-20; 28:9-22; 30:1-17; 31.* Isaiah, as has already been remarked, had a vocabulary of images shared by other prophets, and like them he took pains to point out facts that his "business-as-usual" fellow-Jerusalemites did not want noticed: Before their eyes foreigners were pillaging the fields they once had plowed, and "Zion is left like a hut in a vineyard,Like a shed in a melon patch, like a city blockaded" (1:7-8; NAB). To the solid citizens who thought that they had greased the palms of enough deities and despots so that when the hurricane came their way they would be out of reach, he replied with an answer from on high that transmuted Amos' humble handyman's image into lofty poetry: "Now I shall lay a stone in Zion, a granite stone, a precious corner-stone, a firm foundation-stone: no one who relies on this will stumble. And I will make fair judgment the measure, and uprightness the plumb-line. But hail will sweep away the refuge of lies and floods wash away the hiding place" (28:16-17; NJB).

That kind of talk has usually tended to make the movers and shakers nervous, so poets and visionaries have seldom been nominated to boards of directors or made cabinet ministers. Hezekiah, astonishingly, gave Isaiah a hearing and allowed him to proffer advice on foreign policy issues. 2 Kings 19 records Isaiah's counsel at the time of Sennacherib's siege of Jerusalem. In his own book Isaiah warned of the folly of playing one great power off against another: "In calm detachment lies your safety, your strength in quiet trust. But you would have none of it; 'No,' you said, 'we shall take horse and flee.' Therefore you will be put to flight! 'We shall ride apace,' you said. Therefore swift will be the pace of your pursuers!" (30:15-16; REB).

Both superpowers were fallible and perishable, Isaiah insisted. Only God could offer real protection, only God would act like a lion growling over its prey, undaunted by anyone banding together to chase it off (31:4).

It is often said that it is not in the nature of prophets to give practical advice that people can make decisions by. How profitable was Isaiah's prophetic advice to Hezekiah? Enough to last the king's lifetime and to keep the kingdom going in spite of Hezekiah's ludicrous and deluded son and grandson. Yet, as Abraham Joshua Heschel has observed, "The prophet is a lonely man. He alienates the wicked as well as the pious, the cynics as well as the believers, the priests and the princes, the judges and the false prophets. But to be a prophet means to challenge and to defy and to cast out fear."

D. *Lord, Keep Us Steadfast in Your Word: Josiah's Reform* (640-608): *2 Kings 22:1 through 23:30*. Judah obtained a reprieve for more than a generation, thanks to the decency and astuteness of Josiah, who was made king at the age of eight after his father's assassination. In his youth and early manhood "he followed the example of his ancestor King David, strictly obeying all the laws of God" (22:2;

GNB). In his mid-twenties, he sent the court secretary to give personal supervision to the work of repairs to the Temple, which was being carried out at that time. There was no imputation that the task was being mishandled; rather the intent was to lend the king's personal prestige to the project. The High Priest, Hilkiah, a man with integrity the equal of Josiah's, responded to the young king's interest by telling the court secretary, "I have found the Book of the Law in the house of the Lord" (22:8). When the book was read aloud to Josiah, he immediately went into mourning, ripping his clothes, on account of the way his forebears had violated the precepts of the book. He ordered the High Priest, the court secretary and other officials to take counsel as to what the book's teachings portended for the future of his people; they spoke with a woman prophet named Huldah, who was a member of the family that maintained the Temple's vestments.

The message from God was not very reassuring: Jerusalem and its people would be punished for their idolatry and disobedience of God's laws, so that "they should become a desolation and a curse" (22:19), but because of Josiah's humbleness before God he would be spared the sight of this catastrophe. On hearing this, Josiah did the best he could for his people. He assembled them in the Temple and made a covenant with God, which the people swore to uphold, that he would keep God's commandments "with all his heart and soul" (23:3; NJB, GNB). He thereupon saw to the destruction and desecration of all the pagan altars, shrines and objects of adoration, doing away with these abominations with a systematic thoroughness that none of his most pious ancestors had dared to employ. And he ordered up a celebration of the Passover in God's honor the like of which had never been held in any previous reign.

Sadly, Josiah's grasp of the exigencies of global politics did not match his sure hand in matters religious. He was well enough aware of the waning power of Assyria: it was this partial vacuum that gave him the leeway to govern his land as he felt right. But he misjudged his own strength vis-à-vis Egypt when pharaoh Neco led an army through Judah so as to aid its erstwhile enemy in a futile attempt to put down a rebellion of the Medes and Babylonians; Josiah tried to stop Neco's forces at Megiddo and was killed in battle. With Josiah's tragic passing, Judah's downfall was not far off.

E. *Give Heart and Soul and Mind and Strength—What the Book of the Law Contained: Deuteronomy 4:1-9, 32-40; 6; 8; 10:12-22; 15:1-11; 18.* Alert readers will have noted that the author of Kings, in his summary assessment of Josiah, used language very similar to that with which Josiah himself pledged allegiance to God's statutes: "There had never been a king like him before, who served the Lord with all his heart, mind, and strength" (2 Kings 23:25; GNB). For observant Jews and Christians, these are familiar words. *Shema, Yisrael, YHWH Eloheinu, YHWH ehadh. . .:* "Hear, O Israel: The Lord our God is the only Lord. Love the Lord your God with all your heart,. . . with all your mind, and with all your strength . . . ." This is known to Jews as the Shema, from its first word in Hebrew, and it is recited as a creed in the synagogue service; for Christians it is the first of the two great commandments, as affirmed by Jesus (the English version cited here, based on Mark 12:29-31, is taken from *The Book of Common Prayer,* 1979). In the Hebrew Scriptures it stands at the heart of the Book of Deuteronomy, whose title in English is derived from a Greek word meaning "second law;" the book refers to itself, however, as "the Book of the Torah" (29:20), and it is virtually certain that Deuteronomy consists in large part of the book of divine teachings with precisely that name that was "found" in the Temple during Josiah's reign.

Although the doctrines of Deuteronomy are presented as a summation of Moses' legacy to his people before their entry into the Promised Land, most scholars are convinced that they are a product of a later age in the people's history and were compiled in a period when the need for religious purification became evident. Immediately after the *Shema,* the teaching insists: "Have reverence for the Lord your God, worship only him, and make your promises in his name alone. Do not worship other gods, any of the gods of the peoples around you. If you do worship other gods, the Lord's anger will come against you like fire and will destroy you completely, because the Lord your God, who is present with you, tolerates no rivals" (6:13-15; GNB).

In the commentary to the authoritative annotated edition of the Torah issued by the Union of American Hebrew Congregations, W. Gunther Plaut and Dudley Weinberg state: "It is not Moses who is the speaker or the preacher in Deuteronomy, although the ultimate inspiration for much that is said in Deuteronomy may well be traced back to him. Nor are the auditors of the Deuteronomic preacher the survivors of the wilderness experience which was about to achieve its culmination in Israel's homecoming." The period directly addressed in Deuteronomy is either that of Hezekiah or, even more likely, that of Josiah himself. Rabbis Plaut and Weinberg continue: "The period of Josiah's reign, like the situation of the Israelites on the Steppes of Moab, was one marked by radical renewal, hope, and change. It too seemed like the fulfillment of a promise and was surely so understood by those who lived through it and attempted to interpret its meaning both at the time itself and in retrospect. . . . In sum, Deuteronomy is the heir of old traditions which it molded in accordance with new social and political needs and did so in a prophetic spirit which gave it the urgency of religious imperatives."

F. *How Mighty Are the Sabbaths: Rules Concerning the Holy Days and Jubilees: Leviticus 23; 25:1-43; 26.* Attention has already been drawn to the fact that Josiah made a point of celebrating Passover with unprecedented pomp. No doubt he also saw to it that the other major festivals of the Israelite religion were purged of pagan accretions and restored to authentic significance. Chapter 23 of Leviticus (the Book of the House of Levi, or hereditary sacerdotal tribe) contains the regulations for observing not only Passover but also Shavuoth (or Pentecost, the spring grain harvest), Rosh Hashanah (the new year, in the autumn), Yom Kippur (the Day of Atonement), and Succoth (the Feast of Booths, the autumn harvest-home festival).

Josiah and his High Priest, Hilkiah, were also obviously convinced of the need to reinstitute the system of Sabbath observances, as Deuteronomy 15:1-11 demonstrates. This was a framework, set forth in Leviticus 23:1-4 and the greater part of chapter 25, whereby not only the seventh day of the week (not to mention a major portion of the seventh month of the year) was set aside for God's purposes, but also the seventh year and the year after the seven-times-seventh year. These sabbath or jubilee years were a sound idea not only ecologically and socioeconomically but also theologically: "Your land must

63

not be sold on a permanent basis, because you do not own it; it belongs to God, and you are like foreigners who are allowed to make use of it" (25:23; GNB). Although chapter 26 of Leviticus sets forth both the benefits in obeying these statutes and the penalties for disobedience, there is, alas, no indication that the system for redress of social and economic imbalances and restoration of the balance of nature spelled out there was ever seriously put into practice, even with the best intentions of reformers like Josiah. Greed almost always manages to subdue principle—a fatal flaw in human nature where Judah was concerned.

G. *The Almond Branch over the Despoiled Land: The Early Prophecy of Jeremiah: Jeremiah 1 and 2; 3:21 through 6:30.* Jeremiah was a child prodigy of a prophet. Son of a priest, Jeremiah was fully aware from his youngest days what dangers awaited anyone who dared challenge the prevailing political and religious order. No wonder he exhibited extreme reluctance when God made it clear to him that his services were required. Jeremiah's earliest prophetic vision was, at first blush, one of loveliness and delicacy—an almond branch in blossom, such as gentle Romeo or raw-nerved Catullus must have glimpsed as youths centuries later in the springtime groves surrounding Verona. But with the budding twig that Jeremiah saw, the fecundity portended doom. "The word of the Lord came to me, saying,'Jeremiah, what do you see?' And I said, 'I see an almond limb.' Then the Lord said to me, 'Well seen, for I am limber and alert: I shall see all monitions of mine come to flower'" (1:11-12; paraphrase). God told the stripling, "Look, today I have set you over the nations and kingdoms, to uproot and to knock down, to destroy and to overthrow, to build and to plant" (1:10; NJB). Seen in this context Jeremiah's almond branch presages the little valley with bright grass that the French teenage poet Arthur Rimbaud envisioned, where a soldier not much older than himself lay nestled, his feet among the flowers, an innocent smile on his lips—and in his side, two red holes. Similar, too, are the day-lilies that comforted the still-youthful Dietrich Bonhoeffer when imprisoned by the Nazis: "their cups open slowly in the morning and bloom only for a day; and the next morning there are fresh ones to take their place. The day after

64

tomorrow they will all be over."

The prophetic images spewed forth from young Jeremiah in a disorganized, unstoppable stream. As would have been only natural in a lad who had only lately undergone puberty and was only just beginning to gain awareness of his own potential and potency, most of his prophecies against Judah and its inhabitants were expressed in terms of sex and bloodshed: "I remember your faithful love, the affection of your bridal days, when you followed me through the desert, through a land unsown," God says to Jerusalem through Jeremiah. But now "you have prostituted yourself with the Strangers under every green tree," done it with the adepts of the fertility cults in fruitlands and vineyards that were rightly God's but were desecrated with fetishes and idols (2:2, 3:13; NJB). God's people have given in to the bestial in their nature, so they will be punished like disobedient beasts through the agency of other animals: "a lion from the forest will slaughter them, a wolf from the plains will despoil them, a leopard will be lurking round their towns: anyone who goes out will be torn to pieces—because of their many crimes, their countless infidelities. . .They are well-fed, roving stallions, each neighing for his neighbor's wife. Shall I fail to punish this?" (5:6-9; NJB).

In the midst of all this tumult of lewdness and violence, God—through Jeremiah—bade the people "remove your abominations from my presence" and "circumcise yourself to the Lord, remove the foreskin of your hearts" (4:1,4). This startling admonition, also demanded in Deuteronomy (10:16), lay at the core of Jeremiah's teaching throughout his career. The Israelites had been circumcised afresh at Gilgal before they penetrated the Promised Land, and this physical mark was there to remind them of their dedication to God whenever they coupled to replenish the nation, but to Jeremiah it was meaningless unless it betokened an inner acceptance of the covenant relationship, a complete openness of one's most intimate self to God. Such shocking utterances were but the first fruition of the passionate and combative relationship in which God, who had captivated him as a youngster, kept Jeremiah enthralled his whole life long.

H. *The Greenery Withers, the Brambles Burn: Nahum 1:1-10,15.*
Nahum was no Jeremiah. His prophecy was a perhaps well-intentioned but definitely short-sighted celebration of the downfall of Nineveh, the capital of Sennacherib's Assyrian Empire. Its opening section is an acrostic hymn depicting God's wrath: "Anger comes slowly to God, but his might is awesome. . . Bestriding the storms and the cyclones, he embroils the clouds with his footfall. . ." (1:1-2; paraphrase).

God may indeed have willed Assyria's dismemberment, but Nahum may have done Judah a disservice by providing its population with the means for gloating over a fallen enemy—for a far worse one was already filling the vacuum of power. This very minor prophet has his defenders, among them Martin Luther (who was in temperament no pacifist): "the book teaches us to trust God and to believe, especially when we despair of all human help, human powers, and counsel, that the Lord stands by those who are His, shields His own against all attacks of the enemy, be they ever so powerful." That is all very well, and Nahum did indeed insist, "Judah, celebrate your feasts, carry out your vows" (1:15; NJB)—in other words, observe the holy days prescribed in God's Torah and render to God what is due. But these behests are precisely what most of the people of Judah saw fit to ignore.

I. *The Mayhem Viewed from the Watchtower: Habakkuk 1:1 through 2:4; 3.* Habakkuk was a prophet far more substantial and worth heeding than Nahum. He represented—and continues to exemplify—the thoughtful, principled person who clearly saw that evil was being done by his fellow citizens and that well-deserved retribution was coming their way in the form of a scourge from abroad: "Their horses are swifter than leopards, fiercer than wolves at night; their horsemen gallop on, their horsemen advance from afar, swooping like an eagle anxious to feed" (1:8; NJB). But how, he demanded, if God is wise and just, could God see fit to countenance retributors who were, if possible, doers of even worse evil than that perpetrated by the first group of miscreants? Habakkuk didn't lack perspective, he had a watchtower he could climb into. The first part of the answer he received was foursquare enough: "You see, anyone whose heart is not upright will succumb, but the upright will live through faithful-ness" (2:4; NJB). But it was the final declaration from on high, "The Lord is in his holy Temple; let everyone on earth be silent in his presence" (2:20; GNB), an answer as enigmatic as the one that would come to Job, that elicited from Habakkuk his odd, tremulous hymn of trust (ch. 3). The American Jewish poet Stephen Berg, who has translated the poetry of Japanese Zen Buddhists, observes that "Habakkuk's primary interest as a minor gem in the dialogue between man and God is in the intensity of its brief vision. It can stand as a model of a moment when a lone man calls out to God and is answered in language which, because of its postrational attitude, seems from the tongue of a far wiser consciousness than ours."

J. *The Towers Will Be Toppled—But Humble People Will Turn to God for Help: Zephaniah 1:1 through 2:3;3.* For Zephaniah the day was at hand when all persons would need to be silent in God's presence, but there was nothing enigmatic about what God would be doing and why. The day would be the Day of Judgment, depicted very much as in the medieval Latin hymn *Dies Irae*, once sung in the Requiem Mass: "Day of wrath! O day of mourning! See fulfilled the prophets' warning, Heaven and earth in ashes burning!" Zephaniah urged his nation to come to its senses "before the burning anger of the Lord comes upon you, before the day when he shows his fury. Turn to the Lord, all you humble people of the land, who obey his commands. Do what is right, and humble yourselves before the Lord. Perhaps you will escape punishment on the day when the Lord shows his anger" (2:2-3 GNB). He held out little hope for Jerusalem's ruling classes. "Its officials are like roaring lions; its judges are like hungry wolves, too greedy to leave a bone until morning. The prophets are irresponsible and treacherous; the priests defile what is sacred, and twist the law of God to their own advantage" (3:3-4; GNB). But God has never left the city, he declared, and justice has not ceased to be delivered to God's people. The toppled towers of other nations should give the unrighteous pause—but alas, the shameless never heed the direst warnings. But all the nations of the world will soon be gathered to feel the force of God's anger; after the judgment has been rendered, peace will reign on Zion.

K. *Sing with Joy to God Our Strength: Psalms 81; 50; 116.* This group of texts from a time of foreboding is rounded out with three psalms of gratitude for God's rescue of his people from the troubles that they have been in—in most cases, troubles that they have brought upon themselves. Psalm 81 is appropriate for a feast day, especially a feast day celebrated according to the reforms that Josiah instituted, for in the midst of the festivities, the thoughtful worshiper hears an "unfamiliar voice" (81:6; BCP). It is the voice of God, reminding the people of all the occasions when they wandered away from the One who repeatedly came to their aid and tried to set them in the right paths. "Oh, that my people would listen to me!" God reiterates, "that Israel would walk in my ways!" (81:13; BCP). The people are admonished in Psalm 81, and in Psalm 50 God prepares to witness the judgment that they are to undergo. They are accused of giving lip service to God's statutes while breaking every one of them. The charge is delivered in open court, and notice is served that God will accept no bribes. But there is a way for all charges to be dropped, for the slate to be wiped clean: "Call upon me in the day of trouble; I will deliver you, and you shall honor me" (50:15; BCP). What could be easier? what could be more impossible?

In Psalm 116 the impossible decision has been made, and the reprieved pours out his or her gratitude to the One who did the rescuing: "I will lift up the cup of salvation and call upon the Name of the Lord. . .I will fulfill my vows to the Lord in the presence of all his people, in the courts of the Lord's house, in the midst of you, O Jerusalem. Hallelujah!" (116:11, 16-17; BCP). In Judaism, this psalm is one that has been sung at the end of the Passover meal; in Christianity it has associations with Eastertide. Dietrich Bonhoeffer, for whom the final cup seemed filled with bitterness until the moment came for him to drink it, expresses the Christian understanding of the gratitude uplifted in this psalm: "The present and gracious God, who is in Christ who in turn is in his congregation, is the fulfillment of all thanksgiving, all joy, and all longing in the Psalms. . .Christ brought in himself the sacrifice of God for us and our sacrifice for God. For us there remains only the sacrifice of praise and thanksgiving in prayers, hymns, and in a life lived according to God's commands."

VIII. JUDAH BROUGHT VERY LOW (608-587 B.C.)

The wolves were inexorably at the gates of Jerusalem by now, but the two riverine superpowers did not deliver the *coup de grace* at once to Judah. Global political concerns and the desire to extract wealth as efficiently as possible from its population dictated the policy of toying with the expiring victim for two more decades.

A. *Vassals and Vacillators: Jehoahaz and Jehoiakim* (608-599): *2 Kings 23:31 through 24:7.* Every dog will have its day, but Josiah's sons Jehoahaz and Jehoiakim were a sorry pair of hangdogs indeed. Even though Egypt was in one of its periodic eras of weakness, what was left of the royal house of Judah was no match for the machinations of Neco, the current pharaoh. Jehoahaz was apparently not tractable enough as a vassal, so Neco took him captive when he had strayed too far north and installed his brother, whom he renamed Jehoiakim, on the throne. Jehoiakim forced his people to pay a ruinous tribute to Egypt for the dubious privilege of having him as their nominal ruler. Along came the rising power in the northeast, the redoubtable Nebuchadnezzar, king of Babylon. Invading Judah and the other small states of the Levant, he compelled Jehoiakim to switch his allegiance to him. This lasted till the Babylonians failed in an attempt to invade Egypt; when they withdrew, Jehoiakim changed sides again. His bravado didn't last long. Nebuchadnezzar was soon back in Judah, his own armies augmented with forces from Syria, Ammon and Moab, determined to put an end to all this vacillation and turncoating once and for all.

B. *The Broken Jar, the Flawed Temple and the Corrupt Court: Jeremiah 7 through 9; 13:15 through 15:21; 18 through 20; 22 and 23; 25:1-11; 26; 36; 45.* As he reluctantly pursued his calling as prophet, Jeremiah incurred the wrath of the religious establishment, much of the secular ruling class, and many elements of the common-folk—and God showed signs of being exasperated with him, too, on occasion. It may be that Jeremiah's quarrel with the Temple authorities began even in the time of Josiah. Jeremiah was nothing if not a perfectionist where religion was concerned, and it is quite likely that

69

the reforms put into practice by the High Priest Hilkiah (who may or may not have been distantly related to Jeremiah's father of the same name) were not thoroughgoing enough to suit Jeremiah. Friction can easily develop between moderate, pragmatic reformers and more idealistic and radical ones. At any rate, by Jehoiakim's day, most of the Temple functionaries and their clients were only going through the motions of observing the deuteronomic standards, and they found it convenient to look the other way when pagan practices—including the appalling custom of child sacrifice—were reintroduced. God made it plain to Jeremiah that all this was intolerable and would bring deadly punishment.

Jeremiah was heartsick at the message he was being compelled to deliver, because he ardently loved his people whose shortsighted, self-destructive ways he so deplored. So he alternated between vehemently articulating God's judgment at the gate of the Temple and pleading with God to relent in his punishment of his people and his insistence on Jeremiah's role as his messenger. God not only would not release him from his prophetic duties (even though God was aware, and made Jeremiah aware, that the prophecy would go largely unheeded), but God also sent a drought as earnest of his intentions for Judah's future. Linked to the drought was a most significant symbolic act that God inspired Jeremiah to perform. Jeremiah was sent to a potter's to learn a lesson from what the potter did with clay when it didn't shape up just right. Then he was told to buy a clay jar, take it to the city gate known as the Potsherd Gate (which led to the Hinnom Valley, where the burnt offerings of children were carried out), break it in front of passersby, and declare God's oracle: "I am going to break this people and this city just as one breaks a potter's pot, so that it can never be mended again" (19:11; NJB). This demonstration got Jeremiah in trouble with the chief of the Temple police, who chained him up overnight.

But Jeremiah was not silenced, and he gave a similar performance at the palace, saying that its beautiful, fragrant paneling would soon become kindling, that the king "will have the funeral honors of a donkey" (22:19; GNB), and speculating that the king's son would turn out to be "a shoddy broken pot. . .a crock that no one wants" and his offspring "hurled into a country they know nothing of" (22:28; NJB).

He then directed his condemnation against the clique of prophets-for-hire who had been peddling predictions of peace-in-our-time and "No disaster will touch you" (23:17; NJB) to the business-as-usual clientele.

When Jeremiah took his message into the inner court of the Temple, proclaiming to all comers that unless they started paying attention to what the genuine prophets were saying, God would destroy the Temple in Jerusalem just as he had the shrine at Shiloh—where Jeremiah's ancestor Eli had raised Samuel, the great judge—he got into serious trouble. The clergy incited the people to form a kangaroo court and put Jeremiah to death for treason. Jeremiah stood his ground, declaring that inasmuch as his message was not his own, but God's, they would be killing an innocent man if they dispatched him. The people began to have second thoughts, and support for Jeremiah came from an unexpected quarter, the elders from the countryside, who reminded the gathering that in Hezekiah's day Micah, a country-man like themselves, had pronounced just such an oracle against the Temple Mount. What had Hezekiah and the leadership of Judah done? Did they put that prophet to death? No, instead they listened, pleaded with God to avert the disaster, and God had relented. Jeremiah also had a protector with considerable influence at court: Ahikam, son of Shaphan, who had been Josiah's court secretary and a leading light in the deuteronomic reform. Thus Jeremiah escaped being put to death, and was merely forbidden entrance to the Temple.

But if the power-brokers thought that this ban would cramp Jeremiah's style they were mistaken. He dictated to his disciple Baruch everything that God had caused him to say so far, and he directed him to go to the Temple on the next fast day and read it to the people. Baruch did so, speaking from the room that belonged to Gemariah, another of Shaphan's sons. Gemariah's own son listened to the reading and reported it at the palace, where his father and other officials who were sons of Josiah's reformist faction were gathered. They questioned Baruch, made him read the scroll to them and then advised Baruch to take Jeremiah and go with him into hiding somewhere safe. They reported to the king what had happened, as duty required and in faint hope that the king might be inspired to take the scroll's contents seriously. He did, but not in the way that they had hoped; he was so incensed by its ardent words that as soon as his secretary had read out a few columns of it the king took his penknife and sliced off the offending text and consigned it to the fire. Little daunted by this royal bookburning, Jeremiah in his safe-house bade Baruch take pen in hand yet again and copy down his prophecies, this time even more complete and unexpurgated than previously. Jeremiah would continue to be heard from.

C. *The Captains and the Kings Depart* (598): *2 Kings 24:8-17*. At Jehoiakim's death, while the Babylonian and allied armies were on the march into Judah, his son Jehoiachin, a mere lad, was made king. Shortly after Nebuchadnezzar laid siege to Jerusalem, Jehoiachin surrendered. He and all the court, both the royal family and leading officials, all the skilled artisans and commercial classes in the land, together with the whole population of Jerusalem, were carried away into exile in Mesopotamia. An unskilled peasant population was left in place in Judah, which would prove to be the source of trouble many years in the future. Jehoiachin's uncle, renamed Zedekiah by Nebuchadnezzar, was installed on the throne as an out-and-out puppet. And Solomon's beautiful Temple was entirely despoiled of its furnishings. *Sic transit gloria mundi:* "thus passes the world's glory."

D. *God's Glorious Presence Abandons Jerusalem: Ezekiel's Initial Prophecies* (between 598 and 587): *Ezekiel 1 through 4; 7:1 through 12:20; 17 and 18; 24*. While Babylon copied Assyria in displacing recalcitrant peoples to prevent their causing disorder on the edges of the empire, it did not disperse them in such a way that their sense of identity and community would be destroyed, as Sennacherib had done to the ten northern tribes of Israel. Judah's populace was settled into cohesive villages of their own along the rivers and canals of Mesopotamia; exile was bitter for them, but their awareness of who they were was not obliterated.

Among the deportees living beside the Chebar watercourse was Ezekiel, a priest of God, an assiduous practitioner of orthodox religion. One day in the fifth year of the exile, he was visited with a mind-boggling vision of God (ch. 1); the apparition of the Sovereign of the universe and the elemental forces of existence so overwhelmed

Ezekiel (3:15) that he was paralyzed and struck speechless (3:24-25). When Ezekiel recovered his faculties he was frightened and appalled by the things God required him to do and say in order to try and coax the banished Israelites (and the scattering that remained in Judah) into reforming their ways and abandoning their rebellion against God's strict but gracious Law.

One of the most distasteful things Ezekiel was ordered to do, so as to dramatize the pending siege of Jerusalem and demonstrate the measures that the whole population of Judah would be driven to in captivity, was to make a dough of assorted grains and bake it where everyone could see him do so on a fire fueled with dried human excrement. He was then supposed to eat only a meager portion of such bread and drink only two cups of water a day for more than a year. "The Lord said, 'This represents the way the Israelites will have to eat food which the Law forbids when I scatter them to foreign countries'" (4:13; GNB).

Ezekiel, who had all his life scrupulously maintained ritual purity, balked at defiling himself in this way; God relented only to the point of allowing him to substitute cow dung (a fuel used to this day by the subproletariat in the Near East, but offensive for obvious reasons to the well-bred). The symbol of nauseating cuisine was one that God would return to several times in making his intentions known to Ezekiel.

The remaining population in Jerusalem apparently were going around saying, "The City is the cooking pot and we are the meat" (11:3; NJB). What they may have meant by this expression is not easy to figure out. One scholar, Moshe Greenberg, understands it as a foolish boast: Jerusalem is "a pot being filled with the choicest morsels...themselves." GNB renders it as meaning that things may be bad, but they could be worse: "we are like meat in [the pot], but at least it protects us from the fire." Other interpreters think them guilty of indulging in excessive pessimism and pathetic self-pity. Whatever they may have thought they meant, God prompted Ezekiel to announce to them that they were mistaken: "This city is like a cooking pot all right, but what is the meat? The corpses of those you have killed! You will not be here—I will throw you out of the city!" (11:7; GNB).

God reiterated the metaphor for Ezekiel to relate to his rebellious people on the very day the siege of Jerusalem began. Not only was the fat in the fire for sure this time, not only was their goose about to be cooked, but the pot itself, which had gone without cleansing for so long that it was corroded with scum and rust, was about to be heated red-hot, which would render it ritually pure once again, although no flame was strong enough to burn the corrosion completely away (24:1-14).

All that God made Ezekiel say and do was painful and humiliating to that decent and above-board man, making him in the eyes of his fellow Israelites not a sage but an apostate and a laughingstock. But God had yet one more crushing blow to deliver to Ezekiel as a sign to his people: God took away the life of the poor man's beloved wife and ordered him not to mourn for her. This was to indicate to the Israelites that "I will take away from them the strong Temple that was their pride and joy, which they like to look at and to visit." (24:25; GNB).

Ezekiel, whose ministry, in Temple and out, was his mainstay, knew that this worst of all catastrophes was imminent: in a spirit-led, visionary journey to Jerusalem, he had been brought to see the glory of God's presence—appearing much as it did in the vision which ushered in his prophetic commission—arise from the Holy of Holies in the Temple, depart from the Temple precincts, and quit the once-holy city altogether (ch. 10; 11:22-23). Thus passes the glory of God from a world that made God's presence intolerable. Yet in departing from Jerusalem God assured Ezekiel that he would be present with his people in their exile. Some day, when they had learned to abandon their idolatry, he would let them return to their land. In an oracle that Jeremiah would parallel, God declared through Ezekiel: "I shall give them a single heart and I shall put a new spirit in them; I shall remove the heart of stone from their bodies and give them a heart of flesh, so that they can keep my laws and respect my judgments and put them into practice. Then they will be my people and I shall be their God" (11: 19-20; NJB). But not now, not yet.

E. *The Wooden Yoke and the Iron Collar: Jeremiah's Prophecies during the Last Days of Jerusalem: Jeremiah 24;27 through 31.* Back in Jerusalem, the deportation of the former officialdom has enabled the reappearance of Jeremiah and the resumption of his prophetic mission. Jeremiah, too, was visited with a culinary vision from God. He was shown two baskets of figs placed in front of the Temple. In the question-and-answer format that was a hallmark of God's private messages to Jeremiah, the prophet was made to understand the significance of the two baskets: the good, early-ripening figs were the portion of the people who were in exile in Babylonia—these God would plant, albeit in alien soil for the time being, and would bring to fruition; the figs too bad to eat were those who remained in Judah or had fled to Egypt—these would be uprooted and tossed away (ch. 24).

Jeremiah was inspired to restate this basic message to the remaining Jerusalemites and their leadership in a vivid way. On the occasion of a state visit from ambassadors of the neighboring puppet regimes to their fellow-marionette Zedekiah, Jeremiah trussed himself up in an ox-yoke made of wood and leather and served notice on the controlling interests in Judah and the other Levantine states that those who subjected themselves to Nebuchadnezzar and served him faithfully would survive, but those who rebelled would be driven out and destroyed. For Nebuchadnezzar was acting as God's servant in bringing this subjugation.

To the people of Judah he delivered a further message: Don't believe the false prophets who were predicting that the treasures which had been stripped from the Temple would soon be returned by Babylon and then all would be right as rain. No way, said Jeremiah (ch. 27). This led to quite an altercation in the Temple between Jeremiah and a shyster prophet from Gibeon named Hananiah (the Gibeonites always were a shifty lot). After a slanging match between the two, Hananiah reached over, yanked the yoke off Jeremiah's neck and broke it in pieces, declaring, "The Lord has said that this is how he will break the yoke that King Nebuchadnezzar has put on the neck of all the nations; and he will do this within two years" (28:11; NJB). Jeremiah was for the moment nonplussed and walked out, but he was soon back with the perfect squelch: Hananiah might be able to break a wooden yoke, but God will replace it with an iron yoke. It is reported that Hananiah died in the seventh month—that is, right around the Day of Atonement!—of that very year (28:11).

Jeremiah then used the impending embassy to Nebuchadnezzar of his remaining friends at court (sons of Josiah's reformist party) as an opportunity to send a message of solidarity to the Israelite deportees in Babylonia, the gist of which was what God had imparted to him and he had made public in Jerusalem. He was then himself the subject of a letter of protest sent by one Shemaiah (evidently a bitter and recalcitrant displaced person in Mesopotamia) to Zephaniah, the second-ranking priest at the Temple: Why wasn't he doing his duty by putting an iron collar and chains on that no-good ranter and raver Jeremiah? Jeremiah had a ready retort to this: neither Shemaiah nor any descendant of his would live to see any of the good things that will eventually come out of the Babylonian captivity (29:24-32). This turn of events caused God to reward Jeremiah by commissioning him to make a written record of all that God had revealed to him about the future, when he would "restore my people, Israel and Judah," when he would "break the yoke that is around their neck and remove their chains" (30:3,8; GNB).

Jeremiah seized this opportunity to express not only his sorrows but also his hopes, in some of his most poignantly exultant poetry: "hear the word of the LORD, O nations, proclaim it on distant coasts, and say: He who scattered Israel, now gathers them together, he guards them as a shepherd his flock. The LORD shall ransom Jacob, he shall redeem him from the hand of his conqueror. . .My heart stirs for him, I must show him mercy, says the LORD (31:10-11, 20: NAB). But the peroration went even further: "The days are coming, says the LORD, when I will make a new covenant with the house of Israel and the house of Judah. . .I will place my law within them, and write it upon their hearts" (31:31,33; NAB).

"Jeremiah may not indeed have started out with the conviction that hope could only follow on the crashing of the city walls, but with it he surely ended," Sheldon H. Blank, the Reform Jewish scholar, has observed. "He called for constancy and devotion to God, for faithfulness and a willingness to listen. But he addressed 'uncircumcised hearts' and could not be heard—so that he despaired of communicating, ever. . .Jeremiah did not see anger in the eyes of God; he saw love—and sorrow. He did not see God casting his people off; he saw God letting his people go, regretfully relinquishing his hold. God was surrendering his people; although it cost him pain he was permitting a stubbornly heedless people to destroy itself."

F. *No Stone Left Standing on Another: 2 Kings 24:18 through 25:3. Jeremiah 21; 32; 37:3 through 39:2. 2 Kings 25:4-21. Jeremiah 39:11-18.* Jerusalem came to be destroyed because pseudo-king Zedekiah got too big for the britches the Babylonians had dressed him in. He itched to show his equally pusillanimous neighbors that he was nobody's tool, so when he thought the time was ripe he cut a deal with Egypt, the forerunner of today's "mutual-defense pacts" between a great power and a nonentity. Some deal; Nebuchadnezzar came down in force, and pharaoh looked the other way. Jeremiah was in Jerusalem, a political prisoner confined to the courtyard of the royal palace because he had spoken out against the futile pact with pharaoh.

His eyewitness account of the siege is, to say the least, extraordinary. He leaves no doubt that Zedekiah and the self-serving officials who had pricked the king into defying Babylon were both infuriated by him and afraid of him because he kept turning out to be right. Especially vexing must have been his act of civic protest in buying land back home in Anathoth from his cousin Hanamel, who obviously needed the cash in these wartime conditions. Jeremiah's gesture served notice that he knew that the Babylonians, who were occupying the territory around Anathoth, were people of integrity who would honor a contract, while Zedekiah and his courtiers patently were not. No wonder the latter contrived to get rid of Jeremiah; how he was rescued is a touching story involving Ebedmelech, an African. After the city walls were breached and the Temple was entirely dismantled by the Babylonian army, God not only saw to Jeremiah's safety, but that of the kindly Nubian as well.

IX. BY THE WATERS OF BABYLON (586-538 B.C.)

What can it have felt like to be in exile alongside the Babylonian watercourses after the fall of the city where the Sovereign of the universe was wont to dwell? Singers and seers have railed against the desolation and banishment brought on by warfare, from the plains of ancient Troy--

> *Strength stoops unto the grave,*
> *Worms feed on Hector brave,*
> *Swords may not fight with fate.*
> *Earth still holds ope her gate;*
> *Come! come! the bells do cry.*
> *I am sick, I must die.*
>> *Lord, have mercy on us!*
>
> (Thomas Nashe: "Adieu, farewell earth's bliss")

--to the trenches and death-camps of our own times. But never was the outcry raised with such bleakness and bitter immediacy as in the words of the deportees from Jerusalem.

A. *How Can We Sing upon an Alien Soil? Psalm 137.* It is significant that although the Israelites before the Babylonian captivity and the Jews after it have evidenced a liking for great cities—and Babylon was truly a magnificent one, girt by lofty walls pierced by gates ornamented with enameled bas-reliefs of strutting lions and other proud beasts, and crowned with the ziggurats later known in fable to the envious Greeks as the hanging gardens reckoned to be one of the seven wonders of the world—barely a word of Babylon's splendor is to be found in the texts that the exiled people of Judah composed during this time of utter bereavement. It is as if their eyes could focus only inward on the emptiness of grief and hatred that wracked their vital organs.

Psalm 137 is often thought of as an elegy of haunting beauty. So it would be if it ended with the remembrance of Jerusalem being placed above the singer's highest joy. But it does not end there; it ends on a discord, on notes of vituperation, with an ugly cry for vengeance to be visited not upon their oppressors but upon their children. Rabbis of later eras, troubled by the tone of this psalm, hastened to explain that

God forbade such vengefulness to be executed upon the common people of Babylon, only upon their rulers. Be that as it may, the name of Babylon remained for Jews the label by which they would vilify any city and culture that earned their contempt. And as the poet John Hollander has discerned, "Hanging the harps...on the trees, abandoning familiar and consoling music, is hardly anything but a violent gesture—it is a slamming down of the piano lid, say, or a closing of the instrument case."

B. *Mopping-up Operations: Jeremiah 40:1 through 44:14.* This time, Jerusalem was completely emptied of its population by the Babylonians. However, the commanding officer, Nebuzaradan, did not include Jeremiah among the prisoners to be sent off to Mesopotamia, but treated him with kindness and respect, allowing him to go wherever he pleased. The prophet chose to join his long-time protector Gedaliah, who had been appointed governor of the vanquished territory. From Mizpah, which had been made the administrative headquarters, Jeremiah could minister to the few people who were allowed to remain in the land, mostly subsistence farmers, herdspeople or workers in various enterprises too lucrative for the Babylonians to shut them down.

Jeremiah did not have much time in which to aid his bedraggled fellow remnants, though, because there were several bands of Judean soldiers and their officers who had contrived escape from Jerusalem during the final days of the siege and avoided capture by the Babylonians. These had been roving as irregulars or had found refuge in Transjordan. Gedaliah appealed to them to give themselves up under an amnesty; most did, but one Ishmael, a man about whose intentions Gedaliah had been warned, assassinated the governor and then went on a rampage of bloodletting.

Another irregular, Johanan, thereupon did away with Ishmael, but he was hardly an improvement. Such scum of the earth repeatedly have surfaced in the Near East, carving out niches for themselves in other people's flesh. Even today, their sort—sometimes holding highest offices of state—contrive to stymie any attempt to resolve the region's manifold conflicts. The fact that they seldom last long does not make their depredations any the less grievous.

Jeremiah did what he could for the hapless ordinary folk who were at the mercy of Johanan and his fellow officers, but he was unable to persuade these self-appointed champions that it would prove fatal to carry out their plan of seeking sanctuary in Egypt. "As a shepherd picks his clothes clean of lice, so the king of Babylonia will pick the land of Egypt clean and then leave victorious," God had Jeremiah warn. "He will...burn down the temples of the Egyptian gods...None of the people of Judah who are left and have come to Egypt to live will escape or survive...No one will return except a few refugees" (43:12-13, 44:14; GNB). That is the last to be heard from Jeremiah, down among the fleshpots of Egypt—for which his nation periodically longed and which he utterly despised. He tried nonetheless to bring them what comfort he could along with the unadulterated Word of God. He most likely never got to go home to the land he had bought at Anathoth; he never got to plant any almond trees and watch them come to flower.

C. *All You Who Pass This Way, Look and See: Lamentations 1 through 3; 5.* These dirges for fallen, desolate Jerusalem have not lost their power to move people to shock and pity. The city itself cries out, "is any sorrow like the sorrow inflicted on me...?" (1:12; NJB). But the poems are far from a crying-jag, a wallowing in self-pity. The singer knows that Jerusalem has herself to blame for what has happened to her: "Jerusalem has sinned so gravely that she has become a thing unclean." She is portrayed as one whose self-indulgence has changed her from a person of dignity to a streetwalker too far gone to know how to keep her private parts from being exposed or to control her excretory functions: "Her filth befouls her skirts—she never thought to end like this" (1:8-9; NJB).

Yet the power in this poetry lies not just in such facing up to ugly realities but more especially in the links it courageously forges with worthier eras in the city's past and with utterances of the prophets to which the city turned a deaf ear but which now echo like a banshee's wail among the ruins. In the glory days of Solomon did God's love for Zion seem like the ardor of a young stag staring through the lattice (Song of Songs 2:9)? Now, "from the daughter of Zion all her splendour has departed. Her princes were like stags which could find

80

no pasture" (1:6; NJB). Did Jeremiah wear a yoke in the Temple to warn Jerusalem of what would come upon her if she persisted in enslaving herself to false gods and her own base appetites? This is now acknowledged: God's "yoke is on my neck, he has deprived me of strength" (1:14; NJB).

What is more, the singer slowly starts to gain a proper perspective: "The Lord's love is surely not exhausted, nor has his compassion failed; they are new every morning, so great is his constancy. 'The Lord', I say, 'is all that I have; therefore I shall wait for him patiently'" (3:22-24; REB). No wonder, then, that the language of the poetry soon devolves into a passacaglia and fugue on the theme of atonement. The prayer of confession in the service for the Day of Atonement reads: "Our God and God of our fathers, let our prayer come before thee; hide not thyself from our supplication . . . We have turned aside from thy commandments and good judgments, and it hath profited us nought. But thou art righteous in all that is come upon us." But the singer of Lamentations cannot yet bring himself to such a response, he doesn't yet see his way through to the clear reality of God's justice: "We have sinned and rebelled, and you have not forgiven. You have covered us in anger, pursued us, and slain without pity; you have covered yourself with cloud beyond reach of our prayers" (3:42-44; REB). The song does not yet resolve itself, it does not return to the tonic that would serve as a healing draught. But some day, perhaps, the words of confession will be found appropriate, so that absolution can be given and received, and a new life can begin.

D. *You Have Fed Your People with the Bread of Tears: Psalms 74; 79; 80.* Here is a triad of psalms which are the hymns of angry sinners in the hands of a God who is chastening them to try and make them sin no more. Often when one knows that one is in the wrong, one is tempted to insist that the fault is everyone else's but one's own. The children of Israel indulge themselves in this temptation in these ugly songs. Whose misbehavior brought about the trashing of Mount Zion? Look at somebody else: "the enemy has laid waste everything in your sanctuary. Your adversaries roared in your holy place." (74:3-4; BCP) Blame the foe. Blame the negligent leadership. "There are no signs for us to see; there is no prophet left; there is not one among us"

(74:8; BCP). No Ezekiel? No Jeremiah? Well, how can you take anybody seriously who goes around with an ox-yoke on his neck?

Above all, blame God. Blame God for sending prophets who act like fools, than make one feel foolish for not listening to them. Blame God for letting one's adversaries call one a fool: "We have become a reproach to our neighbors, an object of scorn and derision to those around us" (79:4; BCP). Blame God for not listening to the people who really matter: "O Lord God of hosts, how long will you be angered despite the prayers of your people?" (80:4; BCP). Not until the next to last verse of the last of these psalms does the carping and crabbing cease and a worthy prayer emerge: "give us life, that we may call upon your Name" (80:17; BCP).

One of the few commentators to confront these psalms honestly, from within the community of faith, examining what they really imply about God's people and the perspective from which—until redemption is unequivocally sought—they are doomed to view their God, is Daniel Berrigan. In the note he appends to his own challenging paraphrase of Psalm 74, he writes: "Evil overwhelms us because we stand within the so-called problem, up to our necks, like the guilty in Dante's inferno. We miss our plight precisely because it is our own, not a 'problem' at all, not 'out there,' in a malfunctioning universe, but here, now, under this skin, in this skull, wrought by these choices. We are good consumers, even while we question 'the system' which feeds our appetites like captive animals, on the hour."

So, to ask, "How long will you be angry, O Lord? Will your fury blaze like fire for ever?" (79:5; BCP) is to avoid facing up to the real question, says Berrigan. "No, the real question, the question which appalls and puts to silence, the question which is avoided in principle and neglected in fact, the question for which is substituted every trick of technology, every nostrum of psychology, all the airy and groundless rules of 'religion'—the real question seems to me quite simple. For instance: what is a human being? And how may we become human once more, in a bestial time?"

E. *"Our Redeemer" Is Your Name from of Old*: Isaiah 63:7 through 64:12. At last, some true perspectives have begun to appear in the viewpoint of the people of God, some sense of proportion, some awareness of how vast and timeless almighty God is, yet how timely and precise his redemptive acts have always been on behalf of his people. But here is a prophet speaking, a person who in the degradation of exile, aware that "We have all been like unclean things and our upright deeds like filthy rags" (64:6; NJB), has troubled himself to learn from the oracles pronounced by Isaiah of Jerusalem and has sought to become worthy of inheriting his mantle. He has realized that the first obligation, in the midst of despair, is to "recount the Lord's acts of unfailing love. . .and his great goodness to the house of Israel, all that he has done for them in his tenderness and by his many acts of love" (63:7; NEB).

Only when one is willing to acknowledge the uniqueness of God, to affirm that "Never has ear heard or eye seen any other god who acts for those who wait for him" (64:4; REB), does one dare ask God to try again and reform the botch that one has made of oneself: "we are the clay, you the potter, and all of us are your handiwork" (64:8; REB). It is within that admission that the believing community can affirm: "You come to meet those who are happy to act uprightly; keeping your ways reminds them of you" (64:5; NJB).

"It is true," Abraham Joshua Heschel has said, "that the commandment to be holy is exorbitant, and that our constant failures and transgressions fill us with contrition and grief. Yet we are never lost . . .Despite all faults, failures, and sins, we remain parts of the Covenant. [God's] compassion is greater than His justice. He will accept us in all our frailty and weakness. . .On the other hand, we are constantly warned lest we rely on man's own power and the belief that man, by his power alone, is capable of redeeming the world. Good deeds alone will not redeem history; it is the obedience to God that will make us worthy of being redeemed by God."

X. THAT HE MAY RAISE, THE LORD THROWS DOWN

With the passage of time, existence began to appear less hopeless to the Israelites held captive in Babylonia. In virtually the only reliable historical notice about the life of the Judean exiles provided in the Bible, it is reported that Amelmarduk (called Evilmerodach in the scriptures), shortly after he acceded to the throne of Babylon, released king Jehoiachin of Judah from the prison where he had been held for 37 years, "treated him kindly and gave him a position of greater honor than he gave the other kings who were exiles with him in Babylonia" (2 Kings 25:28; GNB). This generous treatment is symptomatic of the prestigious positions that Israelites had attained in the royal court (also attested to in the legends preserved in the Book of Daniel), where their intelligence and business acumen stood them in good stead. Though there were undoubtedly periodic attempts (fomented by the Babylonian clergy who were chafing under the royal family's efforts to keep their power in check) to coerce the Israelites into paying homage to the Babylonian deities (the worship of whom faithful Israelites dismissed as "star-gazing"), the descendants of Abraham and Sarah were for the most part free to continue to worship the God of their ancestors.

The more perceptive among them winnowed the records of their past, especially their prophetic heritage, to determine how and where God's word of truth had been made known to them, in order to discern what God's intent was for them in the future. In fact, that future was looking brighter for the remnants of Judah than for their Babylonian captors. Amelmarduk was a capricious ruler who lasted only three years before being assassinated. Four years of turmoil followed him before Nabonidus came to the throne in 556 B.C. In the middle years of his reign he made his son Belshazzar co-regent. Evidently this unpopular ruler found expeditions to distant regions of the realm and dabbling in religious eclecticism more to his taste than the mechanics of governance. Many of the inhabitants of Babylonia, both indigenous and transplanted, were ready to welcome the new man of power in the region, King Cyrus of Persia, when he conquered Babylon in 539 B.C.

Cyrus was one of those rare despots in human history—among

them, Alexander the Great, Julius Caesar, Charlemagne and Elizabeth I of England—who combined a well-honed intellect, daring and astuteness in statecraft, personal charisma, and popularity with a broad range of their subjects. The Greek historian Herodotus, who gives a fascinating and lurid account of his birth and rise to power in the first book of his *Histories*, labelled Cyrus "the bravest and most popular young man in Persia" during the period when he was consolidating his power, and leaves no doubt that as a conqueror he was exceptional in his leniency and tolerance toward the vanquished. Small wonder that, according to a surviving Babylonian document, the Babylonian clergy and people were convinced that Cyrus was a liberator who came to them at the behest of their presiding deity, Marduk:

> *Marduk, the great lord, a protector of his people...beheld with pleasure his (i.e. Cyrus') good deeds and his upright mind . . .(and therefore) ordered him to march against his city Babylon. . .Without any battle, he made him enter his town Babylon. . ., sparing Babylon. . .any calamity. . .All the inhabitants of Babylon. . .bowed to him (Cyrus) and kissed his feet, jubilant that he (had received) the kingship. . .*
> (*Cyrus Cylinder*; trans. A. Leo Oppenheim)

No doubt the prophet known to modern scholarship as Second Isaiah was not the only Israelite exiled in Babylonia to share the enthusiasm of the native Mesopotamians for Cyrus. That visionary was, at least at first, willing to declare that none other than the Lord of hosts, the Holy One of Israel, had anointed Cyrus for his conquering and liberating task.

A. *On the Watch for a Revived Israel: Ezekiel 33 and 34: 36:16 through 37:14; 39:21-29; 40 and 41; 43:1-12.* News of Jerusalem's downfall brought renewed impetus and power to Ezekiel's prophetic commission (33:21-22), and people at last began to flock to Ezekiel's house to listen to him, but for the most part they went there because it was the thing to do, not because they had any real idea of what his words meant, much less any intention of heeding them (33:30-33;

85

God in fact compares Ezekiel to a pop singer—like Joan Baez, Bob Dylan or Paul Simon in the 1960s or Bruce Springsteen, John Cougar Mellencamp and Tracy Chapman more recently—whose songs contain trenchant social commentary, but whose audience for the most part just tends to listen to the tune or sway to the beat). Nevertheless, God reiterated his appointment of Ezekiel as watchman over the Israelites' existence (33:1-20). The commissioning to this task of a priest who had felt himself compelled against instinct and training to break the food laws and other such taboos in order to shock people into attending to his message was an important step in the renewal of God's people.

Ezekiel was to be a watchman not in the sense of a sentry on the city walls, like Habakkuk, but like a shepherd's helper at the edge of a grazing herd, wary of approaching marauders. Helper is the operative word, for God was finished with the traditional "shepherds" who were given the task of guarding Israel: "I, the Sovereign Lord, declare that I am your enemy. I will take my sheep away from you and never again let you be their shepherds." David, the founder of the dynasty and champion of the cultus, had been a shepherd in the literal fact and then in metaphorical guardianship of the well-being of the whole nation. His successors, with only a very few exceptions, only looked after their own hides. "I will rescue my sheep from you and not let you eat them" (34:10; GNB). God stated unequivocally to Ezekiel that he intended to take care of his people personally, separating the sheep from the goats, and the strong sheep from the weak (34:17-22).

What God meant, then, by promising his people that "I will give them a king like my servant David to be their one shepherd, and he will take care of them" (34:23; GNB) would remain an enigma for some time to come. For Ezekiel's day and age it was sufficient for them to know of God's gracious clemency as their sovereign: "I will once again let the Israelites ask me for help, and I will let them increase in numbers like a flock of sheep. The cities that are now in ruins will then be as full of people as Jerusalem was once full of the sheep which were offered as sacrifices at a festival" (36:37-38; GNB). The time when the carcasses of God's strays and weaklings would lie abandoned in the recesses of the pasturage would soon be no more. For God led Ezekiel on a spiritual journey into a valley where the ground was covered with bones. In any age of human history this is a grisly vision; for generations which have witnessed the mounds of skeletons in Hitler's extermination camps, or the killing fields of Idi Amin, Pol Pot and various military juntas or insurgents in Latin America, or the bleak graves in the "Bantu homelands" in South Africa, it is an unbearable one. For that very reason it is the one God chose to impress Ezekiel and all who would listen to him with the awesomeness of what God was prepared to do to revive his people. Their selfishness and waywardness had brought exile and immolation upon them, their flesh had been stripped away, their very marrow was desiccated and atomized, so that the wind whistled through the hollows of their bones, but out of this annihilation God would bring new life (37:1-14).

Finally, God granted Ezekiel a vision of the new and ideal Israel, and its Temple first and foremost, which God was prepared to usher in (chs. 40-41). Though the prophet was enjoined to make everything that he had seen in this ultimate vision known to the people, this spiritual glimpse of the renewed Temple must have seemed a personal reward, too, after a ministry that had involved the deliberate violation of the holiness code that meant everything to him. And while the specifications of the sanctuary are set forth in mind-numbing detail, it is clear, as the scholar James Luther Mays points out, that "the purpose was not to provide a blueprint for builders . . .The meticulous measuring of the holy area is the visual objectification of the promise that God would dwell in [the people's] midst forever. . .The theological center of the vision lies in the announcement of the divine demand: the Holy dwells with the people that they may be holy (43:7-10)."

B. *God Saw That It Was Good: The Later Account of Creation and Human Origins* (probably formulated in this period): *Genesis 1:1 through 2:4.* As precisely demarcated as the dimensions of the Temple in Ezekiel's vision is the scenario depicting the formation of the universe and its contents and creatures—especially humankind as the acme of God's creative intent—which is placed first in the Book of Genesis but is believed to be the less ancient of the two accounts provided there. Many scholars are convinced that this narrative was given more or less its present delineations by God's faithful interpreters at the time of the Babylonian captivity partly because the cosmology it presents resembles that discerned by learned astronomers of Nebuchadnezzar's time and place, but more especially because the divine truths which it affirms were ones that God's people needed to be made aware of and be reassured by in that situation.

Dietrich Bonhoeffer has specified the way in which God's people in the midst of defeat and uncertainty needed to be reminded of the goodness of all that God has purposed and accomplished: "God sees the world as good, as created—even where it is the fallen world—and because of the way God sees his work and embraces it and does not forsake it, we live. That God's work is good in no way means that the world is the best of all conceivable worlds. It means that the world lives completely in the presence of God, that it begins and ends in him and that he is Lord."

C. *Was It Not Foretold You from the Beginning? Prophecies of Second Isaiah, a Prophet of the Exile in Babylon* (delivered between 546 and 538): *Isaiah 40:1 through 41:20; 43:1 through 44:20; 45:1-13; 47 and 48; 51:1-16; 52:7-12; 54:1 through 56:8; 57:14 through 58:12; 59.* "Comfort, give comfort to my people, says your God" (40:1). How long the exiles had been waiting to hear such bracing words! "Say to the cities of Judah: Here is your God!. . .Like a shepherd he feeds his flock; in his arms he gathers the lambs, carrying them in his bosom, and leading the ewes with care" (40:9,11, NAB).

Now the message was being delivered to them with power and unforgettable beauty. Who was the messenger? Nothing at all is known about him, apart from what he was inspired to say and that he chose to conceive of his utterances as an extension of the prophecy of Isaiah of Jerusalem. That spiritual forebear, nearly two centuries previously, had foreseen a day when "the remnant of Israel. . .will stop relying on the man who strikes them and will truly rely on. . .the Holy One of Israel" (10:20; NJB). He was certain that "a day is coming when the people will sing, 'I praise you, Lord! You were angry with me, but now you comfort me'" (12:1; GNB). Now, in the perception of the anonymous exile in Babylon who had studied these words assiduously and patterned his own thoughts upon them, that day was about to dawn.

Scholars have noted in Second Isaiah (as he is usually called) "the way in which he returns again and again to Isaiah's way of utterance," but, as Martin Buber has remarked, "there is more than simply that. Isaiah's images are shaped into an ingenious manifoldness; Isaiah's basic conceptions are modified, elaborated in their innermost potentialities, and, so to speak, made dynamic, and it is done so that a path leads from variation to variation and so on, and the uncovered wealth of the basic conceptions is only on this path made completely perceptible."

What are some of the permutations that Second Isaiah has wrought in his mentor's message, the changes he has rung on the major Isaianic themes? Paramount among them is his concept of the Holy One of Israel. It is his contribution to induce his people to observe both the infinite and the infinitesimal workings of God's will simultaneously, and to understand these as pertaining to them in a particular, liberating and redeeming sense. First the immeasurable aspect: "Do you not know? Have you not heard? Was it not foretold you from the beginning? Have you not understood? Since the earth was founded He sits above the vault of the earth, and its inhabitants are like grasshoppers"—so tiny and transitory do they appear from so far aloft (40:21-22; NAB).

Then the intimate aspect: "He gives strength to the fainting; for the weak he makes vigor abound. Though young men faint and grow weary, and youths stagger and fall, they that hope in the LORD will renew their strength, they will soar as with eagles' wings" (40:29-31; NAB).

Then the particular aspect: "fear not, Jacob you worm and Israel poor louse. It is I who help you, says the Lord, your ransomer, the Holy One of Israel" (41:14; NEB). And the lesson to be drawn from these three dimensions? Stated in universal terms: "Who was it that made this happen? Who has determined the course of history? I, the Lord, was there at the beginning, and I, the Lord God, will be there at the end" (41:4; GNB). Stated in particularist terms: "People will see this and know that I, the Lord, have done it. They will come to understand that Israel's holy God has made it happen" (41:20; GNB).

This way of viewing God ("likening" God is what the prophet calls it: 40:25) has several crucial implications for Israel's behavior then and there and for all people of faith at any time and place. First, and in general: "No need to remember past events, no need to think about what was done before. Look, I am doing something new, now it emerges; can you not see it?" (43:18-19; NJB). This is not a license to ignore the record of God's saving acts in history; far from it. It is a command to interpret the salvific events in the light of the present and the future. But this means precisely the need to abandon the hoarding of past injuries and the constant rehearsal of past sins. Redemption is valueless otherwise. Next: "I am the first and I am the last; there is no God except me. Who is like me? Let him call out, let him affirm it and convince me it is so; let him say what has been happening since I instituted an eternal people" (44:6-7; NJB). Thus, the commandment to worship no other gods is to be seen no longer in terms of choosing the all-powerful God over against a deity of lesser might, but in terms of the folly of becoming obsessed with something manufactured, with a nonentity. To do such a thing is to put oneself in a state of absence from God—that outer, utter darkness which would be Jesus of Nazareth's concept of hell.

A similar futility is the kind of selfish utopianism which considers that the world would be a far better place if only one's destined lot had been different: "Does the clay ask the potter what he is doing? Does the pot complain that its maker has no skill? Does anyone dare say to his parents, 'Why did you make me like this?' The Lord, the holy God of Israel, the one who shapes the future, says: 'You have no right to question me about my children or to tell me what I ought to do!'" (45:9-11; GNB). Therefore, the Jerusalem to which the Holy One of Israel is bidding his people return is not to be renewed according to human plans but in line with God's purposes; Zion is to be a holy hill that is both particularly Israel's and open to all: "my house shall be called a house of prayer for all peoples. Thus says the LORD God, who gathers the dispersed of Israel: Others will I gather to him besides those already gathered" (56:8; NAB).

The Jesuit paleontologist and theologian Pierre Teilhard de Chardin has provided what may usefully be regarded as a restatement of Second Isaiah's dynamic of the infinite, the infinitesimal and the particular in contemporary terms: "In each one of us, through matter, the whole history of the world is in part reflected. And however autonomous our soul, it is indebted to an inheritance worked upon from all sides—before ever it came into being—by the totality of all the energies of the earth: it meets and rejoins life at a determined level. Then, hardly has it entered actively into the universe at that particular point than it feels, in its turn, besieged and penetrated by the flow of cosmic influences which have to be ordered and assimilated ...We have not, in us, a body which takes its nourishment independently of our soul. Everything that the body has admitted and has begun to transform must be transfigured by the soul in its turn. The soul does this, no doubt, in its own way and with its own dignity. But it cannot escape from this universal contact nor from that unremitting labour. And that is how the characteristic power of understanding and loving, which will form its immaterial individuality, is gradually perfected in it for its own good and at its own risk. We hardly know in what proportions and under what guise our natural faculties will pass over into the final act of the vision of God. But it can hardly be doubted that, with God's help, it is here below that we give ourselves the eyes and the heart which a final transfiguration will make the organs of a power of adoration, and of a capacity for beautification, particular to each individual man and woman among us. . .Beneath our efforts to put spiritual form into our own lives, the world slowly accumulates, starting with the whole of matter, that which will make of it the Heavenly Jerusalem or the New Earth." (*The Divine Milieu*, I: 3. B.)

D. *Songs of "My Servant, My Chosen One"*: *Isaiah 42:1-7; 49:1-7; 50:4-10; 52:13-53:12.* There is another crucial embellishment of the Isaiah tradition that was a product of the experience of captivity in Babylon. This is the transmutation of the promised Messiah from the powerful Davidic heir whose banner will rally the nations, into a servant entrusted with the carrying out of God's will. The Servant will arouse hatred and strife, and expend all his energy in seeming futility in the effort to perform his appointed task. He will patiently bear insult and injury for the sake of God. He will succeed in his task, but only after taking upon himself the punishment unto death which had been destined for the people whom he served.

This figure is compellingly presented in the four so-called Servant Songs which strangely and hauntingly irrupt into the text of Second Isaiah. Scholars differ as to whether they are from the same inspired mind and hand as the new perspective of the Holy One of Israel or are the insight of yet another peruser of Isaiah's legacy among the exiles. In any case, they expressed for Israel's survivors a stunning new vision of how God's light was to be manifested to the nations "so that all the world may be saved" (49:6; GNB).

Scholars and explicators have often explained away these poems by reckoning the Servant to be either Israel collectively, or some identifiable historical figure of the prophet's own time, or as a merely supernatural figure who will come at the end of the age. None of these explanations would do for the latter-day Hebrew prophet Martin Buber, who has argued that in order to enlarge the vision of the exiled Israelites as to the revealed ways of God "it was necessary to set up over against the inadequate servant, Israel, the anonymous servant, who has been 'chosen' and 'held' as Israel but unlike Israel was one in whom YHWH also delighted, and upon whom He put His Spirit (42:1). . .The stubborn is contrasted with the submissive, the timid with the bold, the blind with the enlightening, and for all this God calls both of them without distinction 'my servant'. . .and promises to both of them His protection, His assistance, and the future gift of His bliss." Nevertheless the extraordinary, unusual servant, who is a real person "standing in a quite peculiarly close relationship to Israel," is there, according to Buber, so that God may say to him, in Israel's hearing, "'*Thou* art the Israel in whom I glorify myself.'"

It is in these four Servant Songs that Judaism and Christianity touch one another most closely as intimately related biblical faiths. From the first disciples on, Christians have of course identified Jesus of Nazareth as the personification of God's Servant. Buber, as a faithful Jew, sees the possibility of the Servant being embodied in a succession of persons who willingly take upon themselves the Servant's prophetic, expiatory and purifying role.

The two perceptions need not be mutually exclusive. Jews, while withholding acknowledgement of Jesus as a Person of the eternal Godhead, are not prevented from seeing him as one who took upon himself the servanthood which brought God's light to the nations.

Christians do not vitiate the uniqueness of Jesus as the Christ by acknowledging a line of willing servants of God leading to and from him, for Christians have long been bidden to the "imitation of Christ." As Thomas a Kempis has written in this regard: "If you wish to be no longer a lover of yourself, but stand ready to do my will. . .you would greatly please me, and your whole life would pass in joy and peace . . .[should you] put off worldly wisdom and all desire to please other people or yourself. I have said, take for yourself what humans ordinarily despise rather then what they value highly. For true heavenly wisdom, not thinking highly of itself nor seeking earthly glorification, is [commonly] perceived to be of small account and almost negligible; many pay it lip service but hold themselves aloof from it in their lives."

E. *No Lions Will Be There: Other Songs from the Book of Isaiah: Isaiah 14:3-20; 12:1-6; 35.* The texts which reveal the variety of ways in which God made known to his people, while still captive in Babylonia, the possibility of a new beginning, are rounded out with three songs found elsewhere in the Book of Isaiah which depict the promise of liberation in a rather more mundane fashion than the Servant Songs. In chapter 14 there is a far from altruistic song of jubilation over the downfall of the king of Babylon and the defeat of pagan religion. Chapter 12 is a straightforward hymn of thanksgiving for the end of God's anger toward Israel, looking forward to a return to Zion. And chapter 35 is a charming song about the "Road of Holiness" leading to Jerusalem—a way edged with blooms, utterly unlike the lion-guarded portals of Babylon.

XI. THE FORTUNES OF ZION RESTORED
(538-around 336 B.C.)

Shortly after his conquest of Babylonia, Cyrus did away with his predecessors' policy of uprooting the more unruly of the subject peoples and resettling them in unfamiliar territory. According to a surviving archival document:

> *I returned to (these) sacred cities on the other side of the Tigris, the sanctuaries of which have been in ruins for a long time, the images which (used) to live therein and established for them permanent sanctuaries. I (also) gathered all their (former) inhabitants and returned (to them) their habitations.*
>
> (*Cyrus Cylinder*; trans. A. Leo Oppenheim)

This was the opportunity the Children of Israel had been awaiting for three quarters of a century. Did they make the most of their opportunity? The following group of texts, all of which are concerned with the return of the deported Judeans to Jerusalem and its surrounding regions, helps provide an answer. (It should be understood, however, that the chronology provided in the biblical texts is muddled and contradictory; the following treatment is based on the views of a majority of scholars, but it is by no means the only possible solution.)

A. *Those Who Sowed with Tears Will Reap with Songs of Joy: Psalm 126.* The King James Version rendered the initial phrase of this psalm in this way: "When the Lord turned again the captivity of Zion, we were like them that dream." Nowadays, scholars are less sure that the psalm is that direct a reference to the return of the Judeans from their exile. It is widely believed to be a hymn for the New Year festival, when the people were anticipating the sowing of new seed and the difficulties sometimes encountered in tending the new crop. In any case, the returnees immediately faced the necessity of providing food for themselves, which involved reestablishing their title to their ancestral soil and becoming reacquainted with the agronomy of the Holy Land, a different one indeed from that of the Tigris-Euphrates basin. As the Methodist scholar Elmer A. Leslie has observed: "Sowing is a difficult business. It takes blood, sweat, and tears to make a farmer. But to the psalmist sowing is the ground of hope. If Israel would reap, Israel must sow. The psalmist possibly had in mind the great words of his Israelite pioneer Hosea: 'Sow to yourselves in righteousness; harvest in proportion to kindness' (10:12). If Israel sows, Israel will reap—not merely the harvests of grain for the New Year, but harvests of national character, stability, and advancement."

B. *They Set the Altar in its Place* (537-515): *Ezra 1; 2:64 through 5:1. Haggai 1:1 through 2:9. Zechariah 1:1 through 4:5, 10b-14; 5:1 through 6:8; 7 and 8. Ezra 5:2 through 6:18.* Whoever compiled the books of Ezra and Nehemiah (originally one work) left something to be desired as an historian. The American Jewish novelist Jay Neugeboren describes his narrative style as "a voice that is individual and passionate and exacting—a voice that mingles passages of the deepest personal feeling with passages that might have been set down by an earnest CPA." That is a generous assessment: the compiler has left awkward gaps, glossed over important matters, rewritten imperial documents to conform to his own pious notions, supplied statistics that are padded or just plain wrong, and given only one side—the one that he supported—of all disputes. He was not so much a clerk as a cleric, and a very narrow-minded one at that.

Be that as it may, it seems that within the first year of Cyrus' reign over the conquered Babylonian domains, a party of Judeans, headed by Sheshbazzar, who had been appointed governor of the territory, returned to Jerusalem and other cities and towns of Judah, each person heading for his or her ancestral region. By no means all the Judeans in Babylonia made the journey or wished to. Tribal chieftains and religious leaders headed the expedition of returnees. Ostensibly, their first task was to rebuild the Temple. The altar of sacrifice was re-erected, and the Temple rituals were reinaugurated. When the foundations for the Temple were laid, says the account, the older persons present wept (perhaps because the new edifice was to be far more modest than Solomon's resplendent one), while the younger people shouted for joy: "No one could distinguish between the joyful shouts and the crying, because the noise they made was so loud that it could be heard for miles" (Ezra 3:13). Anyone who knows how freely emotions are expressed in the Near East would recognize the verisimilitude in that observation!

Less than excited, however, about the return of the Judeans and the rebuilding of the Temple were the people who had been living in the land or in the adjacent territories while the elite of Judah were in exile. Some had never left; others had drifted back over the years as refugees from Egypt or Mesopotamia; still others, like the Samaritans to the north, were a mixed breed of people whose ancestors had been relocated in the region by the Assyrians and had intermarried with indigenous stock, both Israelite and non-Israelite. The Judean leadership viewed all such people with disdain and suspicion, and when some of them approached Zerubbabel, a grandson of Jehoiachin, and offered to lend a hand in rebuilding the Temple, they were rudely rebuffed (4:1-3). Understandably, they resented this rejection, and they used what influence they had at the Persian court to get the work on the Temple stopped. That, at least, is the excuse given for the fact that by the second year of the reign of Darius I (i.e., 520 B.C.), construction had been at a standstill for some time.

Two prophets, Haggai and Zechariah, intervened to try to get things moving again. Haggai gives the distinct impression that the Jerusalemites found whatever royal interdict there may have been against rebuilding the Temple quite convenient, for they certainly had made their own houses comfortable in the meantime. But lately there had been a drought and short harvests, and Haggai interpreted these reversals as indicative of God's displeasure at the Temple's neglect. Haggai reminded them that the wealth that had furnished their dwellings was not theirs: "The silver is mine, and the gold is mine, says the Lord of hosts" (Haggai 2:8).

Zechariah's intervention was more high-flown—apocalyptic, in fact—but the gist of it was the same, with an added appeal to those still resident in Babylon to escape from there and hasten to Jerusalem to join in the rebuilding effort. For God was to make Jerusalem his dwelling-place, and many nations would soon "come to Jerusalem to worship the Lord Almighty and to pray for his blessing. In those days ten foreigners will come to one Jew and say, 'We want to share in your destiny, because we have heard that God is with you'" (Zechariah

8:23; GNB). Zerubbabel, who seems by this time to have been made governor, and Joshua son of Jehozadak, who apparently was High Priest, were encouraged by the prophets' eloquence to recommence construction. There was a short hitch, while Persian officials determined whether there was a royal warrant for re-establishing the Temple, but by 515 B.C. the new House of the Holy One of Israel was completed.

C. *You Shall Call Your Walls Salvation: Prophecies of Third Isaiah: Isaiah 60 through 62.* The exuberance felt by the more idealistic of the returned Judeans at the completion and dedication of the new Temple is magniloquently displayed in the prophecies of Third Isaiah, a seer and poet who undoubtedly had been a disciple of Second Isaiah in Babylon and had been a part of the retinue of returning religious leaders. In the first of these poems, the dispersed of Israel and the wealth of the nations are seen as streaming in to Zion simultaneously to furnish the abode of the Holy One of Israel and bring into being God's reign on earth: "I will make your overseers peace and your taskmasters righteousness. Violence shall no more be heard in your land, devastation or destruction within your borders; you shall call your walls Salvation, and your gates Praise" (60:17-18).

The second poem, which Jesus of Nazareth would quote in initiating his earthly ministry (Luke 4:18-19), is a declaration of a spiritual Jubilee Year (see Leviticus 25:8-12), "a year of favor from the LORD and a day of vindication by our God" (61:2; NAB). It would not be necessary to engage in such mundane pursuits as the tending of herds and vines: Israel's holiness would so impress other nations that "Strangers shall stand ready to pasture your flocks, foreigners shall be your farmers and vinedressers" (61:5; NAB). And the third poem is an epithalamium, a spiritual wedding-paean about Jerusalem as God's Spouse. The city is portrayed as a kind of wedding canopy for the Messiah to enter as the bridegroom of Zion: "Pass through, pass through the gates, prepare the way for the people. . .See, the LORD proclaims to the ends of the earth: Say to daughter Zion, your savior comes! Here is his reward with him, his recompense before him," the blood-guilt money which he brings as Redeemer being transformed into a bride-price (62: 10-11; NAB).

John L. McKenzie, the Jesuit theologian, has noted Third Isaiah's particular concern over "the failure of the community" which has returned to Jerusalem "to regenerate itself morally. This prophet does not mention cultic lapses; he is concerned entirely with the sins of man against man. Indeed, he seems to believe that only a theophany, an inbreak of the divine power and righteousness, will remove the barrier to salvation" thrown up by human obstruction, not least on the part of priestly and Levitical rigorists who have fenced the worship of God off from those who do not meet their tests for cultic purity. "No Old Testament writer says more clearly that the difference between Israelites and Gentiles must disappear in the fullness of Israel."

D. *We, God's Servants, Will Arise and Build: Nehemiah 1 through 4; 6:15 through 7:4; 12:27-47.* Nehemiah was a Jew who had been serving as wine steward to King Artaxerxes in the Persian capital of Susa when he was informed that the walls of Jerusalem were still unrestored and the returnees were experiencing difficulties. He persuaded Artaxerxes to give him a commission to repair the walls, and he set about doing so. These passages are excerpts from his eyewitness account. Certain details of his narrative deserve special attention. For instance, the section of the ramparts near the Persian governor's residence was built by "Melatiah from Gibeon. . .and the men of Gibeon" (3:7; GNB); Nehemiah was not squeamish about having part of the walls built by these not-quite Israelites. Even more interesting is the fact that the daughters of Shallum, warden of one of the Jerusalem districts, helped their father with the sections assigned to him (3:12); so much for women's place being in the home. Which makes all the more ludicrous the refusal of some of the leading men of Tekoa—where the no-nonsense, bare-fisted Amos came from—to sully their hands with manual labor (3:5)! This enterprise understandably incurred the hostility of Sanballat, identified in a document found in Egypt as governor of Samaria, and the leaders of Ammon and the Arab tribes, who devised an aborted plot to assassinate the enterprising former courtier. These details place Nehemiah's mission in the period of 445-443 B.C.

E. *Ezra Had Set His Heart on Carrying Out God's Law* (some time after 433 B.C.): *Ezra 7; 8:15 through 10:16. Nehemiah 8 and 9; 10:28-39.* Nehemiah was rewarded for his efforts in building the walls of Jerusalem by being made royal governor of Judea. However, according to the account in the Book of Ezra, a scholar of the Torah named Ezra obtained from king Artaxerxes in the seventh year of his reign (i.e., 458 B.C.) a commission to refurbish the Temple, renew the purity of its cultus by supplying it with priests who were properly Levitical, and restore its ritual laws. If this date is correct, he would have been in effect co-regent with Nehemiah, which, given the latter's go-to-it executive personality, seems unlikely. Many scholars are of the opinion that the dating is wrong, and that Ezra arrived in the 37th year of Artaxerxes' reign (i.e., 428 B.C.) or even later.

At any rate, Ezra was the sort of purist who professed himself aghast to discover how many Jews had intermarried with indigenous peoples of other ancestry; he rigorously set about making them divorce their "foreign" spouses and disown the children of these unions (Ezra, chs. 9-10). He thereupon read out to the people the purified Law of God. "When the people heard what the Law required, they were so moved that they began to cry" (Nehemiah 8:9; GNB). Ezra enjoined them not to mourn, but to rejoice, and he reinstituted the Feast of Booths (Shavuoth), which had been in abeyance. After singing a hymn of confession (9:6-37), including a reinterpretation of Israel's holy history which gives a good indication of Ezra's theological stance, the people made a covenant to uphold the ritual code—including observance of the Sabbath Year—which Ezra had promulgated. Davie Napier states that Ezra "may not have been the giant the Chronicler makes him out to be—a new Moses, the founder of the new nation, and a new Josiah, revealing afresh the law of Moses," but he says that "it is right" that the psalm-prayer of confession offered by him "has been called 'the birth-hour of Judaism,' and that Ezra is commonly called the father of Judaism."

F. O *Ye Spirits and Souls of the Righteous—Exemplary Tales of Daniel and the Three Youths: Daniel 1; 3 through 6.* Communities are not rebuilt by royal decrees, statistics, prophecy and legal codes alone. Households need to be got through the day, children need to be coaxed and comforted, by other sorts of accounts. "Be a diligent lad, be a clever girl, and you can grow up to be like _____. Let me tell you the story." Grains of historical truth get ground up, kneaded, sugared and otherwise served up by calculating aunts and savvy uncles to provide archetypal role-models for the future leaders of the nation. The episodes of the Daniel saga must have been treated in just such a fashion after the return from Babylon before being put to the emblematic, apocalyptic purposes of the Book of Daniel's compiler in the 2nd century B.C. The meta-historical legends of the burning fiery furnace and the lion's den are wonderful ways of conveying the lesson that God's true followers must not betray their faith, no matter what, and that God will be true to those who are true to him. (These stories indeed proved so popular that Greek translators of Daniel embellished them with further legends and provided the three youths with two magnificent songs of praise: "Blessed art thou, O Lord God of our fathers..," and "O all ye works of the Lord...", which continue to grace services of Morning Prayer in Anglican and other churches.)

G. *Esther and How She Fared: Esther 1:1-4, 10-19; 2:5-8, 15-23; 3:1 through 8:17.* The tale of Esther and how she saved her people from destruction is also one which cannot be aligned with the facts of history. Indeed, its narrative style resembles more than a little one of the Tales of the Thousand-and-One Nights that Sheherezade would tell the sultan Shahryar more than a millennium later on in a successful bid to prevent her own doom. It has little or nothing to do with preserving and sustaining faith in God, who is never mentioned in it, but it has brought solace to Jews in many a dark hour of their history, and it certainly bears witness to the valor of Jewish women in perilous times.

XII. IN THE HOUSE NOT MADE WITH HANDS

What of the inner resources of the Israelite people as their external fortunes sank and resurfaced? Where did they find the spiritual wherewithal to endure their captivity in Babylon and to re-establish the Temple and re-edify their temporal lives when they were allowed to return to Jerusalem? It is believed that the synagogue, basically a lay institution, became a central element of Hebraic life during the exile. The pattern of daily recitation of the Torah and study of its meaning, interspersed with the singing of psalms, gave shape and direction to individuals' existence and enabled corporate regrouping in order to confront the world from a posture of cohesive strength. But the Israelites of the Babylonian and post-exilic periods did not rely solely on what their own community availed. Like the wandering Aramaeans who lived before them and the ubiquitous Jews of later centuries, they were keenly aware of their neighbors, not only doing business with them but also helping themselves to their intellectual and spiritual resources. The Book of Job is based on legends borrowed from gentile sources, and the story of Jonah gets much of its poignancy from the fact that Nineveh, the great city which was the target of the prophet's reluctant mission, was the metropolis of Assyria, Israel's longtime enemy.

A. *Test Me, O Lord, and Try Me: Psalms 4; 11, 13; 17; 22; 25; 26; 27; 30; 31; 32; 36; 39; 40; 42; 43; 51; 57; 62; 63; 69; 70; 71; 86; 102; 115; 123; 130; 143; 73.* Things have gone hideously wrong with the environment in which human beings live these days, the Prince of Wales has observed, because of a widespread "denial of God's place in the scheme of things" and a distorted view of human nature. "Man is more, much more, than a mere mechanical object whose sole aim is to produce money," Prince Charles has said. "Above all he has a soul, and the soul is irrational, unfathomable, mysterious." Nowhere is the ambiguity of the human soul more exposed than in the present group of psalms, which comprises one-fifth of the whole Psalter. Intensely personal, utterly devoid of conventional religious decorum, they give vent to the kinds of unkempt thoughts and feelings you might be loath to utter in church or synagogue but would rather "speak

101

to your heart in silence upon your bed" (4:4; BCP). If the nakedly personal faith expressed in these psalms seems foreign to the ways of those who "dwell in prosperity" (25:12; BCP), it is worth remembering that "O for a closer walk with God," a hymn so genteelly sung in many a mainline parish, was the product of its author's wrenching mental anguish. Even more to the point, it was on the language of these psalms that Jesus drew to voice the feelings of utter aloneness (22:1,15) and yet reliance on the Father (31:5) that arose in him when he hung dying on the cross.

B. *I Tried to Grasp the Infinite: Job 1 through 14; 19:23-27; 29 through 31; (32 through 34); 38; 40: 1-14; 42.* The "patience of Job" was no doubt proverbial long before the author of the Epistle of James used the phrase at the start of the Christian era (James 5:11; KJV). His "righteousness" was a household word to the Israelites during the Babylonian captivity (Ezekiel 14:14). Surely these were the qualities the young Black American actor Forest Whitaker (unforgettable in *Platoon* and *Good Morning, Vietnam*) had in mind in naming Job when asked whom he would pick as national leader if he could choose anyone who ever existed. "He stuck by his beliefs, no matter the consequences, because he believed good would prevail. He's an example of integrity, of hope, of optimism."

Fair enough. But just how *patient* was Job, though? Not very, thinks Stephen Mitchell, the American poet and scholar whose recent translation of the Book of Job is the finest version in modern English. "His speeches are a kaleidoscope of conflicting emotions, addressed to [his] friends, to himself, to God. His attitude shifts constantly, and can veer to its direct opposite in the space of a few verses, the stream of consciousness all at once a torrent. He wants to die; he wants to prove that he is innocent; he wants to shake his fist at God for leaving the world in such a wretched shambles." Yet for Mitchell, as for Whitaker, Job is not "primarily a rich man bereft of his possessions and heartbroken over his dead children," but a universal figure. "He has become Everyman, grieving for all of human history. He suffers not only his own personal pain, but the pain of all the poor and despised."

Because its author has made use of an ancient fable as the framework for a profound examination of the meaning of life, with all its attendant and inescapable agonies—a scrutiny expressed in conflict and in supernatural resolution—the Book of Job has often been compared to a Greek tragedy. (Indeed, the poet Archibald MacLeish reworked the story as a modern-dress poetic drama in the 1950s, turning Job into J.B., an organization-man type of C.E.O., and putting into the mouths of his comforters the buzzwords of the era's reigning pseudo-orthodoxies: fundamentalist rant, psychoanalytical cant, and Marxist claptrap.)

There *is* a Greek drama that resembles Job in a number of ways: *Philoctetes,* by Sophocles, which concerns a great hero who had set forth to participate in the Trojan War but was cast away on an island by his companions after he became afflicted with a suppurating, stinking wound—punishment for some unwitting offense he had committed against the gods. Because he possessed a magical bow without which the war could not be won, the Greeks dispatched two "comforters" to get the bow from him by hook or by crook. One of them, Odysseus, could talk rings around any Eliphaz, Bilbad or Zophar and not mean a word of it. The other, young Neoptolemus, straightaway developed real sympathy for Philoctetes and his plight. Unlike Elihu's anger at Job's self-justification, his behavior toward the stricken man was gentle. He would definitely have shared Elihu's view, however, that "it is not the old that are wise, nor the aged that understand what is right" (32:9); notwithstanding this opinion, both youths end up sounding not all that different from their scorned elders!

But where the two stories *are* utterly unlike is in the kind of divine intervention that concludes them. In Sophocles' play, Heracles appears to Philoctetes and says, Look, I had labors to perform and suffering to endure, like you, but I bore them, and their outcome was the winning of immortal merit. So "make your mind up," he says, "to revere the gods. . .For reverence shall not share the death of mortals: be one alive or dead, it cannot be destroyed." In the Book of Job, God replies to Job's self-serving accusations from the midst of a whirlwind:

Who is this whose ignorant words
smear my design with darkness?

> *Stand up now like a man;*
> > *I will question you: please, instruct me.*
> *Where were you when I planned the earth?*
> > *Tell me, if you are so wise. . .*

The Creator proceeds to a revelation of the whole creative process, to which Job at length summons the strength to respond:

> *I have spoken of the unspeakable*
> > *and tried to grasp the infinite. . .*
> *I had heard of you with my ears;*
> > *but now my eyes have seen you.*
> *Therefore I will be quiet,*
> > *comforted that I am dust.*
> (38:1-4; 42:3,5-6; trans. Stephen Mitchell)

An answer that is a question. No answer and yet the only possible answer. The Love which moves the sun and the other stars is in dialogue with the quintessence of dust.

   C. *Like Wind I Go*: *Ecclesiastes 1 through 5:7; 7 through 9:12; 11 and 12.* "Vanity of vanities, saith the Preacher, vanity of vanities; all is vanity" (1:2; KJV). That melancholy refrain is one of many phrases from this oft-quoted book that are paradoxically so familiar that their real meaning is obscured. The word traditionally rendered "vanity" actually means "breath." As Shakespeare's most Ecclesiastes-like character, Vincentio the Duke of Vienna, puts it: "A breath thou art, servile to all the skyey influences that dost this habitation where thou keep'st hourly afflict" (*Measure for Measure,* III:1). Or, more prosaically: "You're only a gust of wind, altering course with each momentary change in the weather, and soon to vanish utterly."

Whoever the author was—traditionally claimed to be Solomon, though one modern scholar suggests that he may have been a man of Davidic descent appointed governor of Jerusalem by the Persians in the 6th century B.C.—he was hardly a "preacher" as that term is now understood; "collector" would be a better translation of what he is called in Hebrew: *Qoheleth*. The man certainly was a connoisseur:

whatever he collected—houses, gardens, farms, livestock, money, power, women—it was only the best. And "it didn't mean a thing. It was like chasing the wind—of no use at all" (2:11; GNB). Not even the wisdom he amassed had much point, he felt. "Oh, I know, 'Wisdom is better than foolishness, just as light is better than darkness. The wise can see where they are going and fools cannot.' But I know that the same fate is waiting for us all" (2:13-14; GNB, alt.). In this vein the Persian Sufi poet Omar Khayyam would one day write:

> *With them the seed of Wisdom did I sow,*
> *And with mine own hand wrought to make it grow;*
> *And this was all the Harvest that I reap'd—*
> *"I came like Water, and like Wind I go."*
> (*The Rubaiyat*; trans. Edward FitzGerald)

So what is to be done? "I realized that all we can do is be happy and do the best we can while we are still alive. All of us should eat and drink and enjoy what we have worked for. It is God's gift. I know that everything God does will last forever. You can't add anything to it or take anything away from it. And one thing God does is make us have reverence for him" (3:12-14; GNB). The Collector was no selfish hedonist, however: "I looked again at all the injustice that goes on in this world. The oppressed were crying, and no one would help them. No one would help them because their oppressors had power on their side" (4:1; GNB). So he advises cooperation: "Where one alone would be overcome, two will put up resistance" (4:12; NJB). Nor was the Collector a curmudgeonly despiser of youth: "Young people, enjoy your youth," he counseled. "Don't let anything worry you or cause you pain. You aren't going to be young very long. So remember your Creator while you are still young, before those dismal days and years come when you will say, 'I don't enjoy life.'" (11:9-12:1; GNB).

Ernest Hemingway drew on Ecclesiastes for the title of *The Sun Also Rises,* the novel in which he expressed the impotence and aimlessness that many in his generation experienced in the aftermath of the senseless, inconclusive First World War. But the modern writer perhaps most fully imbued with the spirit of Ecclesiastes was the English poet A.E. Housman, the pervading bitterness of whose

105

writings—sweetened with delight in youth and concern for the downtrodden—helped many a British, American or Canadian soldier endure the muddy, bloody trenches of that same war:

> *Now—for a breath I tarry*
> > *Nor yet disperse apart—*
> *Take my hand quick and tell me,*
> > *What have you in your heart.*

> *Speak now, and I will answer;*
> > *How shall I help you, say;*
> *Ere to the wind's twelve quarters*
> > *I take my endless way.*
> > (*A Shropshire Lad* xxxii)

D. *An Aboveboard Man Goes Overboard: Jonah entire.* The salty-witted owner of the Whale Inn in Goshen, Massachusetts, used to offer her guests this bit of Yankee wisdom: "When down in the mouth, remember Jonah—he came out all right!" The Book of Jonah is an instructive fable founded upon the career of a prophet, Jonah the son of Amittai, who came from Gath-hepher in Galilee (2 Kings 14:25). The whole world knows that Jonah was the fellow who got swallowed by a great fish. But what was he doing that got him into such a predicament? And what was he supposed to be doing instead? That is where the story's real meaning lies. God had told Jonah to go to the great pagan city of Nineveh and proclaim to it that unless it gave up its wicked ways God would destroy it. Jonah intended to do no such thing. A pious man, he hated Nineveh and everything it stood for; it suited him just fine for it to be wiped out. So he got on a ship bound for Tarshish, at the opposite end of the Mediterranean. Hence the tempest, the frightened sailors, Jonah overboard, and the giant fish.

God once again ordered Jonah to Nineveh, and this time he went and did what he was told. Lo and behold, when Jonah announced God's judgment to the people of Nineveh they took him seriously; "they proclaimed a fast and put on sackcloth, from the greatest to the least" (3:5; NJB). When Jonah realized that God had accepted their change of heart, he was beside himself with anger and slunk off to the edge of town to see what would happen next. God's next action upset Jonah all the more, and God's retort to Jonah's grumbling is the ultimate put-down to self-righteousness, to favoring justice over mercy (4:11).

It is no accident that the Book of Jonah is read in the synagogue on the Day of Atonement. And it should not be missed that Jesus spoke of "the sign of Jonah" (Matthew 16:4) in anticipation of his own atoning death and liberating resurrection—in consequence of which he instructed his followers to "go. . .and make disciples of all nations" (Matthew 28:19). Leopoldo Niilus, the Estonian-Argentine lawyer who formerly headed the Commission of the Churches on International Affairs, has drawn a lesson from the story of Jonah for people of faith today. "One temptation in today's world is to withdraw from the unpleasant realities we see about us, to give up the hope that Nineveh might repent and not be destroyed. Some think, unrealistically, that they can still 'go it alone;' others desire to avoid 'unpopularity,' to be defeatist; or to give in to a pervasive feeling of despair, saying, 'What is the use?'" he writes. "Another temptation becoming more and more prevalent is to produce apocalyptic visions which leave no real hope for repentance and salvation. Indeed, we stand under God's judgment just as surely as did Nineveh, and there are just as few signs for us to justify our being optimistic. God has however promised to save us even from ourselves. Yet we are often tempted, like Jonah, even to hope for the worst! Today, none of us has any need 'to go' to Nineveh. We all live in Nineveh—if not downtown, at least in the suburbs."

E. *Search Me Out, O God, and Know My Heart: Psalms 16; 23; 121; 131; 139.* Many of the themes raised as challenges in the "human predicament" psalms, Job, Jonah and Ecclesiastes are replicated in this group of psalms as affirmations of faith. In the most famous psalm of all, God's awesome power—symbolized by a winnowing flail and a shepherd's crook like those always grasped by the Egyptian pharaohs on their monuments—inspires total confidence (23:4). The relentless turning of days and seasons bodes no unease, when God is in charge (121:6). One may "dwell in the uttermost parts of the sea" (139:8; BCP), yet God is even there, caring for one "like a child upon its mother's breast" (131:3; BCP). Such affirmation of God as "my

107

portion and my cup," as the One sure to "uphold my lot" (16:5; BCP), is not made glibly. Dietrich Bonhoeffer, the German saint martyred by the Nazis, reached for this language when in prison:

Should it be ours to drain the cup of grieving
even to the dregs of pain, at thy command,
we will not falter, thankfully receiving
all that is given by thy loving hand.

F. *Let the Name of the Lord Be Blessed: Psalms 107; 113; 118; 34; 66; 67; 85; 92; 138.* "Blessed is he who comes in the Name of the Lord" (118:26; BCP). These familiar words have different but not unrelated resonances in modern Judaism and Christianity. Jews express this affirmation in the Passover *seder* and at weddings when the bridegroom takes his place under the marriage canopy. The house of Aaron has felt the ungodly encompass them, they were pressed so hard that they almost fell, but God came to their help (118:3,11,13). The Temple has been destroyed, but God ordains that life shall prevail in the tents of the righteous (118:15). And the inheritance of Israel gives thanks. Christians express this affirmation when the One who called himself the Bridegroom takes his place in the way that leads to death for himself but eternal life for those who follow him (Mark 11:9). The Temple of his body may be destroyed, but "the same stone which the builders rejected has become the chief cornerstone" (118:22; BCP. Compare Mark 12:10, Ephesians 2:20). And the inheritance of Israel gives thanks. Whenever the church renders its thanks in the Eucharist for new and unending life through Christ Jesus, it repeats these familiar words.

But it must not be supposed that these words resounded in the ears of ancient Israel as they do to faithful people today. Mitchell Dahood, the Jesuit scholar, bluntly describes Psalm 118—surely the centerpiece of the thanksgiving psalms in the Psalter—as "a king's hymn of thanks for delivery from death and for a military victory." A dusty, blood-drenched battlefield seems a far cry from a wedding tent or the fair linen cloth of the Lord's table. But Shakespeare, who caused his exemplary warrior king Henry V to summon up visions of home and fidelity before the battle of Agincourt, impelled him in victory to order the singing of appropriate psalms and canticles: "Do we all holy rites: Let there be sung *Non nobis* and *Te Deum*" (*Henry V*, IV:8, referring to Psalm 115 and the canticle, "You are God").

What Henry Plantagenet, as Shakespeare envisioned him, shared with his Davidic counterpart, and what contemporary communities of faith need to recover, was an overt expression of the understanding that—as the Anglican scholar Harvey H. Guthrie, Jr., describes it— "the Old Testament conception of thanksgiving is not abstract, nor is it rooted in human attitudes or emotions. Its meaning lies in God's gracious action, in *his* deliverance of his devotee, in *his* salvation. It is a setting forth of God's action, a witness to his victory over the powers of chaos."

XIII. MY THOUGHTS WERE STEADY, SO I WAS READY WHEN TROUBLE CAME (around 330-50 B.C.)

The era of tranquility that the Jews experienced under Persian hegemony was not ended when Alexander the Great conquered Persia and seized its empire in 334-330 B.C. Tutored in the most up-to-date Greek philosophy by none other than Aristotle, the young Macedonian king was tolerant and eclectic in his religious views; legend has it that the High Priest of the Temple in Jerusalem headed a welcoming procession when Alexander passed through the Holy Land in 332. After his untimely death, his Ptolemaic successors in Egypt and—for a while—the Seleucid rulers of Syria continued his benevolent despotism in matters spiritual and temporal. The Jews prospered economically and established communities in Alexandria, Antioch and beyond, to the extent that in the 1st century B.C. the Greek geographer Strabo wrote that "it is difficult to find a single place in the world in which this tribe has not been received."

For the most part it was also a period of intellectual and religious development for them. Their encounter with Hellenism, the Greek philosophical and aesthetic ethos that had followed in Alexander's wake, stimulated a search for wisdom on the part of Jewish thinkers wherever they might find it, sometimes in perusing the writings of others but most often in re-examining their own tradition. Trouble came, however, after the Seleucids replaced the Ptolemies as overlords of Judea. Antiochus IV Epiphanes, who assumed the throne of Syria in 176 B.C., made the imposition of Hellenism on all his domain a state policy. Although some Jews were compliant, many resisted, which provoked harsh reprisals on the king's part: the Temple was desecrated by sacrifices to pagan gods, and Sabbath observance and circumcision were outlawed. A revolt broke out under Jewish leaders known as the Maccabees, who after a protracted struggle secured self-determination and a degree of independence for Judea under Jewish monarchs until the Romans made the territory a prefectorial province in A.D. 6.

A. *He Will Pour Forth Words of Wisdom: Ecclesiasticus (Sirach) 39:1-11*. Preface to this group of texts is a vivid sketch of a seeker after "the law of the Most High," the prototype of a "scribe"—or Hebraic biblical scholar—who "will seek out the wisdom of all the ancients" (39:1) and will become "upright in purpose and learning" (39:7; NJB). One is reminded of Chaucer's clerk of Oxenford in *The Canterbury Tales,* whose clothes were threadbare and who spent every spare coin on books, spoke tersely but with decorum and reverence, "and gladly wolde he lerne and gladly teche;" the scribe's readiness to serve in the courts of rulers and go abroad in foreign lands (39:4) is reminiscent of such wayfarers in the Christian era as Egeria, the 4th-century member of a religious community in Aquitania or Galicia who left an invaluable record of her pilgrimage to Jerusalem, or Benjamin of Tudela, A Navarrese Jew of the 12th century, who wrote an equally insightful account of his own journey through the Levant. "Much have I travell'd in the realms of gold, And many goodly states and kingdoms seen," sang John Keats of the expanse of wonder and discernment open to those who devote themselves to the pursuit of knowledge beyond the mundane.

B. *Give Me Understanding, According to Your Word: Psalms 1, 119: 1-24, 33-72, 89-96, 105-136, 161-176*. Psalm 1, composed some time after the return of the Jews to Jerusalem from their Babylonian captivity, is a beatitude upon those who meditate on God's Law "day and night" (1:2; BCP). Placing this psalm first in the Psalter was a suitable idea, states Charles L. Taylor, because God's will is revealed not only through words of inspiration and wisdom but especially in human relationships shaped by divinely-ordered standards of conduct, and this psalm forcefully presents "two fundamental truths: that the Lord is with the just, and that [whoever] diligently seeks and then follows the divine will is fortunate—not happy in any superficial sense, not merely lucky, but in that right state often described as blessed."

Psalm 119, also a product of the post-exilic period, is the longest poem in the Psalter, comprised of 176 verses. Its subject, too, is the praise of God's law and the rewards to be derived from the study of it. The unique beauty of this paean to the splendor of the divine commandments is seldom revealed in translation, for the stylistic device which its author has employed to enshrine the perfection of God's utterance is an extended acrostic, wherein the initial letter of every verse within each of its 22 sections is the same letter of the Hebrew alphabet, and the sections follow each other in alphabetical order.

Ronald Knox, the English Roman Catholic priest and man-of-letters, made a translation which reproduces the acrostic format. Here is a portion of the third section (119:17-19) in his version:

"Crown thy servant with life, to live faithfully to thy commands. Clear sight be mine, to contemplate the wonders of thy law. Comfort this earthly exile; do not refuse me the knowledge of thy will."

C.S. Lewis, the literary critic and Anglican lay theologian, has likened this psalm to embroidery or to the unique British campanologists' art of change-ringing. J.S. Bach's legerdemain with counterpoint, especially in *The Art of the Fugue*, is yet another example of such a response of human genius to the intricate and flawless beauty of the mind of God.

[C. *The Principles of Piety: from the* Pseudepigrapha: *The Letter of Aristeas 131-168.* Charles, Vol. II, pp. 107-110; Charlesworth, Vol. Two, pp. 21-24; De Lange, pp. 154-157.] "O godly, O beguiling Law!" chants the chorus in Jean Racine's religious drama *Athaliah*, adding that the sweet reasonableness of the Torah makes it impossible not to embrace the faithful love of the God whose ways were manifested to Moses. Nowhere is this attitude better exemplified than in the Letter of Aristeas, a pseudepigraphic work by a Jew based in Alexandria who seeks to convince both fellow Jews living in the diaspora and gentile neighbors with whom he shares a peaceful coexistence that a lifestyle according to the traditions of Judaism is perfectly rational and entirely consonant with the enlightened worldview that any up-to-date person of whatever background or persuasion would opt for (Herman Wouk's *This is My God* was written to serve a similar purpose in 20th-century America).

The bulk of this epistle purports to be a true account of the making of the translation into Greek of the Hebrew Scriptures known as the Septuagint. But one of its principal interests for modern readers is the rationale it contains, supposedly supplied by Eleazar, the High Priest of the Temple, for the laws the Bible sets forth for the faithful to live by: "Our Lawgiver first of all laid down the principles of piety and righteousness and inculcated them point by point, not merely by prohibitions but by the use of [positive] examples as well" (v. 131). For "our Lawgiver, being a wise man and specially endowed by God to understand all things, took a comprehensive view of each particular detail, and fenced us round with impregnable ramparts and walls of iron, that we might not mingle at all with any of the other nations, but remain pure in body and soul, free from all vain imaginations, worshipping the one Almighty God above the whole creation" (v. 139). The "rules of purity, affecting. . .what we eat, or drink, or touch, or see" were enacted "lest we should be corrupted by any abomination," and there is "a deep reason in each individual case" for what foods are allowed and which forbidden (vv. 142-143). The birds and beasts which Jews may eat are of exemplary gentleness in their lives and thus embody the lesson that believers in the one true God "must be just and effect nothing by violence" and avoid lording it over others (v. 148).

Similarly, Jews are enjoined to place the words of God's statutes (in fact, the text of Deuteronomy 6:4-9 and 11:13-21) on their doorposts (v. 158) and also, "when lying down to sleep and rising up again, to meditate upon the works of God, not only in word, but by observing distinctly the change and impression produced upon them" (v. 160), so that they may realize "that we ought to perform every act in righteousness" and "the fear of God" (v. 159). In sum, "nothing has been enacted in the scripture thoughtlessly or without due reason, but its purpose is to enable us throughout our whole life and in all our actions to practice righteousness before all [humanity], being mindful of Almighty God" (v. 168; all extracts trans. H. T. Andrews).

D. *Death before Disobedience: 2 Maccabees 7*. The story of brutality told here, of seven Jewish brothers and their mother who were tortured and then put to death by the Greek king of Syria, Antiochus Epiphanes, for refusing to disobey the Torah, epitomizes

113

the dark side of the encounter between Judaism and Hellenistic culture. Time and again in their subsequent history Jews would be subjected to similar mistreatment for their insistence on maintaining a distinct identity and set of customs that ran contrary to the prevalent norms of the majority population or the ruling elite. The most excruciating example of such anti-Jewish persecution was the Holocaust perpetrated by the Nazis in this century. Humankind's rulers seem to have learned little from that tragic episode except how to acquire the techniques and apparatus of brutality for their own use: torture and genocide continue to be regularly visited upon out-groups in many parts of the earth. The lesson of the Golden Rule, though often stated ("Judge your neighbor's feelings by your own" was the way Ben Sira put it; 31:15), seems to be lost on so many of us— whether we be perpetrators, guilty or innocent bystanders, or even one-time victims.

E. *Wisdom Takes Her Stand in the Streets: Proverbs 1:2-33; 3:1-26; 5:1-14; 7:6 through 9:12.* Ignoring or defying God's precepts can lead to tragedy, and faithfully following them can bring one suffering and martyrdom, as has just been observed. Pursuing God's wisdom can bring one greatness—and there can be moments of comedy along the way, as may now be seen.

The instruction of the young is a serious matter—which can become ludicrous or detrimental with the wrong curriculum, or when in the wrong hands, or when preachment and practice clash. "Do as I say, not as I did when your age" is often the gist of what youth is actually taught by its elders. In return, the young sometimes can't resist mocking their seniors, many of whom they accurately perceive to be merely older—not wiser—than themselves. Still, people manage to learn, and wisdom will out, despite the worst endeavors of the human race.

One of the most ironic demonstrations of the subversive power of wisdom shows up in Shakespeare's *Henry IV* plays when Prince Hal, the heir to the throne of England, goes slumming with that fallen angel of massive avoirdupois, Sir John Falstaff, a corrupter of youth and of anything else he can lay his hands on. Yet Falstaff from time to time enjoys pretending to be young royalty's tutor in the virtuous

114

life: "An old lord of the council rated me the other day in the street about you, sir, but I marked him not; and yet he talked very wisely, but I regarded him not; and yet he talked wisely, and in the street too." The prince tosses this bogus moralizing right back to the old varmint: "Thou didst well; for wisdom cries out in the streets, and no man regards it" (*Henry IV, Part I*, I:2). Young Henry has benefited from conventional tutelage as well as his attendance at Falstaff's night school, for his rejoinder is straight out of the Book of Proverbs (1:20, 24)!

The retort is drawn from one of several sections of wise sayings added in the period of the 3rd-1st centuries B.C. to the aphoristic collection begun in the reign of Solomon. Wisdom is entrancingly described in these passages as a living, breathing entity to be embraced with gusto, though the argument in Wisdom's favor is most compellingly made in this proverbial material through the portrait of her seductive opposite, the personification of Wantonness: "One foolish fellow. . .was walking along the street near the corner where a certain woman lived. . .She was a bold and shameless woman who always walked the streets. . .She threw her arms around the young man kissed him, looked him straight in the eye, and said,'. . .I've covered my bed with sheets of colored linen from Egypt. I've perfumed it with myrrh, aloes, and cinnamon. Come on!. . .' Suddenly he was going with her like. . .a deer prancing into a trap" (7:7-22, excerpted; GNB). Did the stripling escape her clutches? Prince Hal managed to, eventually, and was the better king for his experiences.

F. *A Sage Pays Court to Wisdom and Dispenses Her Gifts: Ecclesiasticus (Sirach) 1:1 through 2:11; 3 through 6; 8:-1-19; 10; 7-18; 14:3 through 15:20; 18:1-14; 19:4-17; 24:1-22; 25:1-11; 27:4-7; 27: 30 through 28:7; 29:1-13; 30: 21-25; 37:7-15; 38:1-15; 40:1-27; 41: 1-4; 42:15 through 45:16 [45:17 through 50:21]; 50:22-24; 51:1-30.* Let the author announce what his book—extensively sampled here—is all about: "Wise instruction, appropriate proverbs, I have written in this book. . .as they gushed forth from my heart's understanding" (50:27; NAB). Yeshua ben Eleazar ben Sira was an instructor of wealthy youths, living, teaching and writing in Jerusalem, putting his thoughts on paper around 180 B.C., just before the imposition of

Hellenism by Antiochus and the subsequent revolt by the Maccabees. His work, which appears to have been widely disseminated in early rabbinic Judaism and in the ancient church, is made up of two major parts.

The first part is a vast compilation of maxims on a wide variety of topics—including duties toward one's parents, charity to the poor, prudence in dealing with others, pride, loose talk, resentment, the selection of one's advisers, the miseries and joys of life, death—all gathered under the overarching truth that, as the proverb says, "the fear of the Lord is the beginning of wisdom" (Proverbs 9:10). Indeed, Nicholas de Lange, the British scholar of rabbinic studies, has shown in his anthology of selections from the Apocrypha, that the first part of Yeshua ben Sira's work is actually a series of little homilies on various biblical aphorisms that were and still are in general circulation; other scholars have demonstrated that Ben Sira drew on a wide range of sources, some of them non-Jewish, in fleshing out his teachings.

His technique may be demonstrated by examining his discussion of friendship: "When you gain a friend, first test him, and be not too ready to trust him. For one sort of friend is a friend when it suits him, but he will not be with you in time of distress. . .When things go well, he is your other self, and lords it over your servants; but if you are brought low, he turns against you and avoids meeting you. . .A faithful friend is a sturdy shelter; he who finds one finds a treasure. A faithful friend is beyond price, no sum can balance his worth. A faithful friend is a life-saving remedy, such as he who fears God finds; for he who fears God behaves accordingly, and his friend will be like himself" (6:7-8, 11-12, 14-17; NAB). Clearly this is an expansion of the famous proverb, "A friend is a friend at all times; it is for adversity that a brother is born" (Proverbs 17:17). That he chooses to express the worth of true friendship in pecuniary terms suggests that Ben Sira may have been familiar with the wisdom poetry of Theognis, a Greek aristocrat of the 6th century B.C. who repeatedly used such imagery:

Few fond companions, lad, you'll find will stay
faithful to you should hard times come your way—
the sort who'll have the passion and the pluck

to share your want as well as your good luck
    (*Elegies*, 11. 79-82).

Yet Ben Sira characteristically relates the topic to his general theme by connecting "fear of the Lord" with genuineness in comradely love. The second part of his book is a long, splendid poem extolling the Most High and "the magnificent works of his wisdom" (42:21; NJB), both as manifested in the sun, moon, stars and other wonders of nature, and as revealed in the history of the human race—especially the deeds of those who have "observed the Law of the Most High, and entered into a covenant with him" (44:20; NJB), the offspring of Abraham. His traversal of the roster of Israel's great leaders concludes with the exhortation: "And now bless the God of all things, the doer of great deeds everywhere. . .May he grant us cheerful hearts and bring peace in our time, in Israel for ages on ages. May his mercy be faithfully with us, may he redeem us in our own times!" (50:22-24; NJB). And as a final flourish, the poet describes in an acrostic his passionate pursuit of Wisdom:

    A s an innocent youth I wooed her.
    B eautifully she came to me: I plumbed her depths.
    C allow youth yielded to ripeness,
    D evotedly I dogged her footsteps. . .
        (51:13-15; trans. Nicholas de Lange)

G. *Wisdom Pervades All Things: Wisdom 1:16 through 3:12; 6:22 through 12:22.* The Book of Wisdom presents itself as the reflections of the Israelite king Solomon, but its actual author was most likely a Jew living in Alexandria, Egypt, in the 1st century B.C. to the 1st century A.D., writing in Greek and making use of certain Greek philosophical ideas while firmly rejecting others. His intended readership was no doubt fellow Jews in the diaspora who were tempted to abandon their ancestral religion for some exotic cult, some belief system that professed itself to own a corner on all truth, or some utterly hedonistic way of life.

The first excerpt, in an echo of Psalm 1, contrasts the attitudes and behavior of the godless with the demeanor and destiny of the upright

117

who seek true wisdom. The author rejects the debased version of the "gather ye rosebuds while ye may" attitude prevalent at the time among pagans (2:8), and he draws a devastating portrait of the power brokers, inside traders and shady real-estate speculators of his day, who think nothing of cheating the poor (2:10) and despise those who spend their time not amassing property but gaining insight into the will of God; any such individual, these fast-laners say "is a living refutation of our designs. His very sight is oppressive to us,. for his life-style is odd, and his ways are weird" (2:14-15; trans. David Winston).

The second passage is an eloquent panegyric to Wisdom, personified as a celestial being existent from before the creation of the universe: "she is so pure, she pervades and permeates all things. She is a breath of the power of God, pure emanation of the glory of the Almighty; so nothing impure can find its way into her. For she is a reflection of the eternal light, untarnished mirror of God's active power, and image of his goodness" (7:24-26 NJB). Clearly this imagery informed Christian conceptions of the eternally-begotten Christ (compare Colossians 1:15-17; John 1:1-5) and of the Holy Spirit.

H. *My Heart Shall Meditate on Understanding: Job 28. Psalms 37; 49; 91; 128.* Rounding out this group of texts upholding devotion to God's Torah and encouraging search for divine Wisdom are five poems counseling respite from tumult and offering solace in times of trouble. Job 28 is a hymn to Wisdom inserted into the dialogue between Job and his would-be comforters. Most scholars consider it a late composition; a few believe it to have been written as a separate work by the author of the Job dialogues. Among the later is Robert Gordis, who summarizes the poem's message thus: "Only God, who created the universe, knows the transcendental Wisdom. As for man, the only wisdom that is accessible to him consists of religion and morality, reverence for the Lord and avoidance of evil."

The four psalms gathered here are masterly offerings of trust and wise counsel. Psalm 37, according to Elmer A. Leslie, encapsules the advice proffered to youth by a worshipful, God-fearing Israelite: "The instruction of this sage-psalmist is based on personal observa-

118

tion. He is now an elderly man and can look back across the years to his boyhood. Throughout his life he has never witnessed a righteous person uncared for, but on the contrary he has seen how gracious and generous the righteous man is to others and how the very remembrance of him is a blessing." Psalm 49 advises all who will listen not to be dazzled by the wealthy, the sybarites, the conspicuous consumers of worldly goods, nor even to be overawed by the wise "who delight in their own works" (49:12; BCP): in the end, death will bring them all down to the grave's common level. "God cannot be bought off," as Charles L. Taylor tartly remarks. Yet the psalmist is confident that "God will ransom my life; he will snatch me from the grasp of death" (49:15; BCP). Psalm 91 is an eloquent song of confidence in God as protector of every believing person. Such a one, says Leslie, has God "as his shelter, his refuge. . . . Security, response, relief, honor, long life, and salvation in its fullest meaning—all this will come to the man who knows God's name." Similarly, Psalm 128, as Mitchell Dahood writes, "teaches that the man who worships the Lord and obeys his commandments is rewarded with a happy and prosperous family." Sings the psalmist: "The Lord bless you from Zion, and may you see the prosperity of Jerusalem all the days of your life" (128:5; BCP).

XIV. GOD'S KINGDOM TARRIES LONG

How shall a nation that is called "the holy people" (Isaiah 62:12) conduct itself? How is it to sustain itself in that role? "Happy is the nation whose God is the Lord!" sings the psalmist, "happy the people he has chosen to be his own!" (Psalm 33:12; BCP). Israel was a people that "proclaimed the Lord of the Word as its only king," Martin Buber has written, "and its legitimate existence was contingent on the condition that it would be ready to consummate this faith in the totality of life."

Such a consummation, though devoutly to be wished, is more easily prescribed than performed. The urge to be ordinary is strong among human beings: it is more tempting to be rich than to be righteous, to be powerful than to be pristine. "To be a good man—sure, we'd all prefer it," avows Peachum in Brecht and Weill's *Three Penny Opera,* "and give the poor our worldly goods, why not? If all are good, God's reign is not far off. Who wouldn't rather dwell in God's own light? . . .But that is simply not the way things are." For as Buber also insisted: "A people which seriously calls God himself its king must become a true people, a community where all members are ruled by honesty without compulsion, kindness without hypocrisy, and the brotherliness of those who are passionately devoted to their divine leader. When social inequality, distinction between the free and the unfree, splits the community and creates chasms between its members, there can be no true people, there can be no 'God's people.'"

The way things were for the Jews in the period from 175 B.C. to A.D. 70 caused many among them to long for God to intervene decisively in the life of their nation. Some, like the Maccabees in the era when the Seleucids of Syria held sway over Judea or like the Zealots during the Roman domination, were convinced that national salvation could be brought about only by rigorous piety coupled with armed insurrection. Others, like the Pharisees and Sadducees, counseled a peaceable but separate coexistence with the foreign dominant power while maintaining careful observance of the Torah's tenets. There were differences between these two parties. The Pharisees believed that one's life is controlled by providential destiny, one's soul survives death and one is rewarded or punished in the hereafter according to one's conduct in the present world. And they taught a devout but nuanced interpretation of the divine Law. The Sadducees believed that free will alone determines the conduct of one's life, there is no world to come, and hence, God's commands must be obeyed strictly and transgressions punished severely.

Still others, like the Essenes, opted to absent themselves from any dealings with unclean foreigners or other Jews who had become corrupted by contacts with them, leading a life of personal and communal purity, devoting themselves to pursuing a knowledge of God's will while awaiting the cataclysmic event which they believed would bring about the end of the age and the establishment of God's perfect rule. The texts grouped here, scriptural and extrabiblical, show some of the ways that these various parties viewed the times which all of them realized were a-changing. God, however, proved to be as unpredictable and unmanipulable as always, and what God would soon cause to take place in the life of Israel was not what any of these factions anticipated.

A. *The Lord, Most High over All the Earth: Psalms 97, 99.* "The Lord is King" is the forthright declaration which begins both of these magnificent psalms. However, they spell out the implications of God's supremacy in different ways. In Psalm 97 the earth is called upon to exult and "the multitude of the isles," whose populations have hitherto been held in the thralls of paganism, are urged to "be glad," because "righteousness and justice are the foundations of his throne" and for that reason God will surely confound "all who worship carved images and delight in false gods" (97:1-2, 7; BCP). The rescue of the heathen from spiritual darkness brings joy to "the cities of Judah" and heightens their security, because it is by making his truth known among the nations that God "preserves the lives of his saints and delivers them from the hands of the wicked" (97:8,10; BCP).

In Psalm 99, the earth is bade to shake, and the people are called upon to "confess his Name" and "fall down before his footstool" because God has "executed justice and righteousness in Jacob" (99:3-5; BCP). The emphasis here is that Israel's own history proves that they can rely for their preservation on the God who "answered them indeed;. . .who forgave them, yet punished them for their evil deeds"

(99:8; BCP). As Mitchell Dahood notes, "The seemingly contradictory attributes of the forgiving and the punishing God can be reconciled. Even in his grace, Yahweh remains a holy God. This means that he severely punishes the sins of men with the same seriousness of the love by which he forgives sin."

B. *Gentile Persecution and Jewish Revolt: 1 Maccabees 1:1-28, 41-63; 2:1-50; 3; 4:1-25, 36-59.* These excerpts contain highlights of a pietistic Jewish chronicler's account of the confrontation between the king of Syria, Antiochus IV Epiphanes (reigned 175-164 B.C.), as he attempted to impose Hellenism on Judea, and the priest Mattathias and his family and followers, known as the Maccabees, as they fought back. The events are recounted in 1 Maccabees exclusively from a Maccabean point of view. Other parties in the conflict certainly would have regarded them differently. There is a bronze portrait statuette of Antiochus in the Nelson-Atkins Museum in Kansas City: his massive body has assumed a heroic stance; the fine features of his face are set in an expression that is at once sensitive and haughty. He spent his youth as a student in Athens and his young manhood as a royal hostage in Rome; he came away from both experiences convinced of the superiority of Greek culture and Roman efficiency. According to Jonathan A. Goldstein, the classical scholar and foremost expert on the Maccabean revolt, Antiochus at first offered Hellenic educational methods and cultural facilities along with Antiochene citizenship to the Jews and other subject peoples as a privilege which, from his perspective, was highly to be prized. Many Jews agreed with him. The "gymnasium in Jerusalem" which they built "according to Gentile custom" (1:14) was no sports palace. It was the centerpiece of an educational method based on the principle of "a sound mind in a sound body;" successful completion of the course of study could lead to far-reaching commercial opportunities and even preferment at court.

Not until a band of Jews attempted a rearguard revolt when he was making war on Ptolemaic Egypt in 169 B.C. did he attempt to impose his ways on the entire Jewish people in the Holy Land. But then he acted with both Levantine fury and Roman ruthlessness. In the Temple, as Goldstein reconstructs what transpired, he installed a triad of deities who were his idea of the heavenly powers which the Jews ought to be worshiping: a sky god (akin to YHWH, and resembling Zeus), a goddess of wisdom (akin to the Holy Wisdom celebrated in the Jewish apocryphal books, yet resembling Athena), and a youthful male god (once slain, but then restored to life, like Adonis). Antiochus' agents shredded and burned any copies of the Torah found in anyone's possession (1:56-57), cruelly abusing and executing all who obeyed its dictates (1:60-61). Mattathias, his sons and other like-minded people organized a resistance; amazingly, they managed to prevail. They cleansed and rededicated the Temple (4:37-59), and secured the independence of Judea under their own rule as High Priests and later as kings. But their zealous methods were as peremptory and unsparing as those of their erstwhile overlord: "Mattathias and his friends. . .forcibly circumcised all the uncircumcised boys that they found within the borders of Israel" (2:45-46). One of his descendants, John Hyrcanus, forced the Idumeans, a neighboring people, to accept Judaism. This was a security precaution that was to backfire: king Herod, mistakenly labelled "the Great," and his offspring were of Idumean ancestry.

The military option and political machinations have never brought the people of Israel the enduring safety and self-determination that they have sought. As Martin Buber has observed, when "one who is serious about his religiousness in any situation whatever, functions in the political sphere, religion is introduced into politics. But the way to the religious goal is essentially dissimilar in its conduct of affairs, its perspective, its manner of going, its tempo, and, lastly, in the unforseeableness, if compared with political conduct. The holy cause of introducing the religious reality into politics runs the danger, therefore, that the categories will mingle, that the goal will become an end, the way a means; that man, instead of treading the path taken by that step of God through history, will run blindly over it. If religion is threatened at one pole by the ice of isolation in which it forfeits a tie with the communal-building human share in the coming of the kingdom, here it is threatened by evaporation in the rapid fire of political activity. Only in the great *polis* [city] of God will religion and politics be blended into a life of world community, in an eternity wherein neither religion nor politics will any longer exist."

C. See What Is Coming to You from God: *Daniel 2; 7; 10 through 12. Micah 4:1-7; 5:1-4. Isaiah 24:1 through 25:9; 26:1-19. Jeremiah 17:5-18. Baruch 4:21 through 5:9.* [*From* The Dead Sea Scrolls: *Apocryphal Psalms Scroll XXII: Apostrophe to Zion.* Vermes, 3rd edn. pp. 212-213; De Lange, pp. 232- 233.] In what manner is the city of God to come about? What would existence be like in a realm founded through God's will and governed according to God's direction? Human beings have long pondered the concept of an ideal state. Philosophers from Plato to Thomas More to Karl Marx have devised their own models of such an entity; dramatists, whether Aristophanes with his Cloudcuckooland, Shakespeare with the "brave new world" of his *Tempest*, or Lerner and Loewe with their mist-shrouded Brigadoon, have demonstrated why a place of that sort could scarcely exist or long endure while men and women remain as they are. When the Hebrew prophets and visionaries were inspired to foresee the reign of God, however, they were not engaging in abstract thought nor indulging in speculation to while away the time. Their purpose was urgent. Unless they could convince their fellow Israelites to change their ways at the prospect of a divinely ordered future, their nation's very existence was in jeopardy. The passages gathered here display the range of insights circulating among Jews of the 1st centuries B.C. and A.D. concerning the irruption of God's kingdom into the human milieu.

Though the Daniel story itself is more ancient, the apocalyptic visions in the Book of Daniel are thought to have been added to it at the time that 1 Maccabees was written, for they appear to comment obliquely on the events of the Antiochene persecution and the Maccabean revolt. Chapter 2 tells of a dream that king Nebuchadnezzar of Babylon had and Daniel interpreted, in which the king saw a gleaming statue, whose head was of gold, whose chest and arms were of silver, whose belly and thighs were of bronze and whose legs were of iron and feet part iron and part clay; before the king's eyes it was struck by a stone, crumbled and was blown away, and "the stone that had struck the statue grew into a great mountain" (2:31-36; NJB). Daniel explains that the statue represents the successive empires of humankind, and the stone stands for the kingdom which "the God in heaven will set up" and "which will never be destroyed" (2:44; NJB).

The original audience would probably have understood the four successive metals to refer to the sequence of great empires from the Babylonian through that of Alexander, with the unamalgamated mixture of iron and clay standing for the unstable and risky political situation of their own day. In chapter 7 the dream is altered to a series of ferocious beasts who terrorize the earth yet eventually pass away, succeeded by a venerable Person enthroned among multitudes of people; to this "Ancient in Years" comes "one like a human being" whose "sovereignty. . .was not to pass away" (7:9-14; REB). Though the imagery has changed—to figures that will reappear in the Revelation to John which closes the New Testament—the meaning is the same.

Finally, in chapters 10 through 12, Daniel himself receives a vision of a man dressed in linen, who predicts the power struggle between the Seleucids and the Ptolemies, the rise to sovereignty of Antiochus Epiphanes and how his forces "will desecrate the sanctuary and citadel; they will abolish the regular offering, and will set up 'the abominable thing that causes desolation'" (11:31; REB). But he assures Daniel that "At that time there will appear Michael the great captain"—that is, the archangel in command of the heavenly forces—and "your people will be delivered" (12:1; REB). What all this signifies, according to Alexander A. Di Lella, the Franciscan scholar, is that "the Kingdom of God which replaces the kingdoms of the godless cannot be inaugurated by military means or purely human resources. . .Yet, paradoxically, men and women of faith are called upon to work mightily for the Kingdom and to respond with conviction and energy to the demands of the Kingdom."

For many centuries the people of Israel had had in their heritage a proclamation, transmitted by both Isaiah and Micah, that "in the latter days. . .the mountain of the house of the Lord. . .shall be raised up above the hills;" the nations of the world will gather there to learn God's ways, "and they shall beat their swords into ploughshares, and their spears into pruning hooks" (Isaiah 2:2-4; Micah 4:1-3).

In Micah's version, all persons will gain the tranquility of self-sufficiency, with their own gardens and groves to tend; and the exiled and the physically or spiritually handicapped, heretofore denied participation in the Temple rites, will be made "the stock of the

125

future" (Micah 4:6-7; trans. J.B. Phillips). Though God's people are momentarily beleaguered, they can look forward to a future "ruler" who will come to them out of Bethlehem "when she who is in travail has brought forth" (5:3); he will be their shepherd and bring them security and peace. One may apply to these eschatological passages in Micah what Peter R. Ackroyd observes of the apocalyptic texts in Isaiah: "The establishment of Zion as central to a newly ordered world is the expression of confidence that it is God alone who will reign supreme."

Isaiah, in 24:1 through 25:9, shows the coming of God's kingdom as taking place in two stages. First, a great leveling, at once geophysical and pandemic: the earth's surface will be wrung and its social order skewed. The world's delights are abolished and its horrors broken down, all of which elicits joy from the majority but grief from the prophet, who notes how the opportunistic and the treacherous thrive in this hiatus, this black hole that negates the balance of the heavenly spheres. But then God surpasses all the wondrous things seen heretofore: the pall that has constricted the nations is removed, and the eternal feast of life is spread out upon God's holy mountain. The hymn of thanksgiving that is then sung (26:1-19) makes it clear that if "our city is strong" this is entirely God's accomplishment: "everything that we achieve is the result of what you do" (26:1, 12; GNB). Indeed, in an ironic parody of the "woman in labor" image, God's people admit in all honesty that their own efforts amounted to no more than a phantom pregnancy, whereas God in the ultimate time of fulfillment makes the earth so fecund that the dead are reborn to life.

For Jeremiah, characteristically, the prospect of God's reign is fraught with ambiguity. The material found in 17:5-18 is hard to cope with: John Bright speaks for many exegetes when he describes it as "heterogeneous in the extreme." But if it is understood to refer in various ways to the Temple on Mount Zion as the core of God's realm, both in the here-and-now and in the messianic age, then it no longer appears to be "the contents of Jeremiah's 'miscellaneous file'" but takes on coherence. Human efforts are utterly unreliable and are as misplaced as "scrub in the wastelands" (17:6; NJB). In his own spin on the motherhood image already found in Micah and Isaiah, Jeremiah suggests that anyone who puts any store in human enterprise alone is as stupid as a partridge who raises the chick hatched from the egg that a cuckoo has laid in its nest: the greedy interloper grabs sustenance that should have gone to legitimate progeny (Aristophanes, author of the satiric comedy *The Birds,* would have chortled at Jeremiah's angry simile; 17:11). God alone is trustworthy. If humanity had heeded God's will in the first place, Zion would not be at risk—"a glorious throne, sublime from the beginning, such is our Holy Place" (17:12; NJB)—and there would be no need for God to intervene to rescue Israel. So damn and blast all who taunt him and say, "Where is the word of the LORD? Let it come to pass!" (17:15; NAB).

Is that any way to pray that "thy kingdom come"? Yes, if you are Jeremiah, says the Reform Jewish scholar Sheldon H. Blank: "These passages suggest that Jeremiah was human. He lacked that form of saintliness which would have required him to forgive his persecutors . . .It may be significant and a clue to his personality that he could at the same time hate persons and love people. What his prayers reveal of furious resentments and unforgiving anger cannot conceal the deeper currents of tenderness in his nature and his involvement with city and nation—with Jerusalem, 'the daughter of his people,' and with Israel, 'God's flock.'"

Jerusalem as both the daughter of God, "who gave you your name," and the mother of "favourite children. . . carried off like a flock by a marauding enemy," is the subject of a psalm of encouragement and hope embedded in the Book of Baruch, a work ascribed to Jeremiah's tutee and secretary but almost certainly written in the early 2nd century B.C. when tensions between the Judeans and their gentile overlords were on the increase but persecution and hostilities had not yet broken out between the faithful of Zion and those "who turned away from the Laws of God," backed by "a ruthless nation speaking a foreign language" (4:30,26,12,15; NJB). Jerusalem is urged to bedeck herself like the royal figure she is intended to be by her maker: "put the diadem of the Eternal One's glory on your head" (5:2; NJB). For, in images now utterly familiar from the prophets of old, all other mountains but Zion will be flattened and fragrant trees will provide shade for the people in God's fertile, well-watered realm. As the scholar Carey A. Moore notes, "the psalm pulsates with a spirit of hope and expectancy—God is on the verge of doing something wonderful!"

The same sense of joyful anticipation infuses the Apostrophe to Zion, hitherto unknown, which was found among several apocryphal psalms in the Dead Sea scrolls: "I will remember you, O Zion, for a blessing; with all my might I love you; your memory is to be blessed forever. Your hope is great, O Zion; Peace and your awaited salvation will come. Generation after generation shall dwell in you, and generations of the pious shall be your ornament. They who desire the day of your salvation shall rejoice in the greatness of your glory, and in your beautiful streets they shall make tinkling sounds. . . . Be exalted and increase, O Zion; Praise the Most High, your Redeemer! May my soul rejoice in your glory!" (Psalms Scroll XXII, excerpted; trans. G. Vermes). This hymn, acrostic in form (and so translated by Nicholas de Lange), is antecedent of such medieval and renaissance Christian hymns as *Urbs beata Jerusalem* and "Jerusalem, my happy home," extolling the city of God where

> *Thy turrets and thy pinnacles*
> *With carbuncles do shine;*
> *Thy very streets are paved with gold,*
> *Surpassing clear and fine*

and

> *Within thy gates nothing doth come*
> *That is not passing clean.*

It is a forerunner of the visionary tradition that would culminate in William Blake's affirmation:

> *I will not cease from Mental Fight*
> *Nor shall my Sword sleep in my hand*
> *Till we have built Jerusalem*
> *In England's green & pleasant Land.*

D. God's Anointed and His Saving Strength: *Joel 2 and 3. Obadiah 15-21. Malachi 3 and 4. Zechariah 9:9-17; 12:1-10; 13:1 through 14:9. [From the* Pseudepigrapha: *Psalms of Solomon 11, 17 and 18.* Charles, Vol. II, pp. 643-644, 647-652; Charlesworth, Vol. Two, pp. 661-662, 665-670; De Lange, p. 231. *Testament of Levi 18.* Charles, Vol. II, pp. 314-315; Charlesworth, Vol. One, pp. 794-795.]
Most Jews and Christians do not need to be told that "Messiah" is an anglicization of a Hebrew word, *mashiah*, which means "anointed." It refers to the fact that the Israelite kings were anointed with consecrated oil, much as British monarchs are to this day, in token of their sacred trust as rulers and guardians of a people dedicated to God. In the psalms and the historical books of the Hebrew Bible the word is used generally to refer to the reigning member of the Davidic dynasty. Thus when prophets and visionaries in troubled times foresaw a Messiah who would deliver Israel, their expectation was of a divinely-chosen man who was "of the house and lineage of David" (Luke 2:4). It was only in the final two centuries before the birth of Jesus of Nazareth that the concept of the Messiah began to assume preternatural or divine dimensions.

Franz Kafka, the Bohemian Jewish author whose disturbing fictions—such as *The Trial* and "The Metamorphosis"—reveal him to be a latter-day heir of the Hebrew prophets, made the bitter jest that the Messiah will come only when he is no longer needed. Be that as it may, the forewarnings of the prophet Joel are entirely appropriate to a creepy world in which one can be changed overnight into something other than human or be arrested and tried for a crime that is never specified. Joel, of whose life and times virtually nothing is known, sees the onset of "the day of the Lord" in the form of a swarm of locusts that inexorably consume everything in their path: "As they leap on the tops of the mountains, they rattle like chariots; they crackle like dry grass on fire. They are lined up like a great army ready for battle" (2:1-5; GNB).

Inevitable as the destruction appears to be, God makes clear that "even now" there is time for Israel to assemble at Mount Zion, opt for repentance, and enable God to shower mercy and insight and plenteousness on his people, as he would prefer. For all other nations the day of reckoning is at hand as well. The universal Judge taunts them

129

with a reversal of the disarmament augured in Micah and Isaiah: "Beat your plowshares into swords, and your pruning hooks into spears; let the weak say, 'I am a warrior.'" (3:10). The nations are commanded to gather in the valley of Jehoshaphat below the Temple Mount: "Multitudes, multitudes in the valley of decision!" (3:14). Once the judgment has taken place, however, "the mountains shall drip sweet wine. . . and all the stream beds of Judah shall flow with water" (3:18).

The oracle of Obadiah (the briefest book in the Hebrew Scriptures) is—if such a thing is possible—even grimmer than Joel's. God's *lex talionis* of "eye for eye" will be applied to the nations in full measure: "As you have done, it shall be done to you, your deeds shall return on your own head. For as you have drunk upon my holy mountain, all the nations round about shall drink; they shall drink, and stagger, and shall be as though they had not been" (vv. 15-16). Obadiah's message, uttered it is not known when, is meant to have a sobering effect on both the Israelites and their hostile neighbors. "The single prophecy of Obadiah which we have", observes the Israeli historian Joseph Klausner, "closes with a Messianic oracle that is political at its beginning and spiritual at its end: 'And saviors shall come up on Mount Zion to judge the mount of Esau; and the kingdom shall be the Lord's'" (v. 21).

Malachi depicts the coming of the Judge and the judgment that he will surely render in shockingly personal terms: "Look, I shall send my messenger to clear a way before me. And suddenly the Lord whom you seek will come to his Temple. . .Who will be able to resist the day of his coming? Who will remain standing when he appears? For he will be like a refiner's fire" (3:1-2; NJB). Because these words are so familiar from the portion of Handel's Messiah that is often sung in the Advent season, the threat which they direct against the prevailing habits of human life is drowned out by jingle bells. God is saying that he has had more than enough of tinsel and is about to find out who is of true gold and silver and who isn't. For God is being cheated by the sorcerers and other religious charlatans, by the "businessmen's Bible fellowship" that manipulates and evades God's statutes in order to "oppress the wage-earner, the widow and the orphan, and . . . rob the foreigner of his rights" (3:5; NJB). Pay your

130

dues, says God, or there will be fire next time. And yet, God reiterates, he is more than willing to spare those who will heed him, for "you have not ceased to be children of Jacob" (3:6; NJB). To the American Jewish novelist Francine Prose, the divine promise as stated here is reassuring rather than threatening: "The ways this love is expressed, the raging, the curses, the impossible demands, seem finally less important than the fact of its eternal endurance."

The messianic prophecies appended to the Book of Zechariah some time in the period of Greek ascendancy sound a note of triumph: "Rejoice heart and soul, daughter of Zion! Shout for joy, daughter of Jerusalem! Look, your king is approaching, he is vindicated and victorious, humble and riding on a donkey. . . . He will proclaim peace to the nations, his empire will stretch from sea to sea" (9:9-10; NJB). An extraordinary divine grace will be poured out over the offspring of David and the inhabitants of Jerusalem to sustain them in the inevitable and cataclysmic conflict with the nations of the earth, amid which "they will mourn for the one whom they have pierced as though for an only child" (12:10 NJB). Christianity has from earliest days understood this passage as predicting the crucifixion of Jesus of Nazareth (see Matthew 24:30; John 19:37; Revelation 1:7), but a passage in the Talmud (Sukkah 52a) also regards it as a reference to the Messiah. In the warfare over Jerusalem, the Lord personally "will sally out and fight" (14:3; NJB). At its conclusion "the Lord will become king over all the earth; on that day the Lord will be one and his name one" (14:9)

In the pseudepigraphic Psalms of Solomon, composed in the 1st century B.C. in reaction to the seizure of Jerusalem by Roman legions under Pompey, messianic expectations are to be found in explicit detail. The violation of the Temple precincts by the troops awakened memories of previous profanations of Mount Zion by gentile invaders. It seemed to the author, as no doubt to many of his contemporaries, that only the advent of the reign of God's Messiah could bring redress. Psalm 11, which has elements in common with Baruch 4:36-5:9, is a song of expectation: "Blow ye in Zion on the trumpet to summon (the) saints, cause ye to be heard in Jerusalem the voice of him that bringeth good tidings; For God hath had pity on Israel in visiting them" (11:1). The children of Jerusalem, who had been scattered among other nations, are assembled from all points of the compass. Jerusalem is to don her holiest vestments. "For God hath spoken good concerning Israel, for ever and ever. Let the Lord do what He hath spoken concerning Israel and Jerusalem; Let the Lord raise up Israel by His glorious name" (11:8-9).

Psalm 17, which is related to the biblical Psalm 72, is the most explicitly messianic of the Psalms of Solomon. "O Lord, Thou art our King for ever and ever, for in Thee, O God, doth our soul glory," the song begins. The psalmist reminds the Almighty, "Thou, O Lord, didst choose David (to be) king over Israel" and swore to him that, as regards his descendants, "never should his kingdom fail before Thee." But owing to the sins of God's people, "sinners rose up against us; They assailed us and thrust us out" of the land of Israel (17:1,4-5). The people entreat the Lord to raise up a king for them once again from the house of David: "gird him with strength, that he may shatter unrighteous rulers, and that he may purge Jerusalem from nations that trample (her) down to destruction"; it is hoped that "He shall destroy the pride of the sinner as a potter's vessel. With a rod of iron he shall break in pieces all their substance, He shall destroy the godless nations with the word of his mouth" (17:22-24). Yet compassion is sought in his judgment of Israel and all the nations: "His words (shall be) like the words of the holy ones in the midst of sanctified peoples. Blessed be they that shall be in those days, in that they shall see the good fortune of Israel which God shall bring to pass in the gathering together of the tribes. . .The Lord Himself is our king for ever and ever" (17:43-44, 46).

Psalm 18 of the Psalms of Solomon somewhat resembles the canonical Psalm 8 in showing the extent of God's goodness to range from the lowliest of mortals to the vastness of outer space: "Lord, Thy mercy is over the works of Thy hands for ever. . .Thine ears listen to the hopeful prayer of the poor. Thy judgments (are executed) upon the whole earth in mercy. . .May God cleanse Israel against the day of mercy and blessing, against the day of choice when He bringeth back His anointed. Blessed shall they be that shall be in those days, in that they shall see the goodness of the Lord. . .under the rod of chastening of the Lord's anointed" (18:1-7). This destiny is as firmly fixed in God's plan as are the stars themselves: "Great is our God and

132

glorious, dwelling in the highest . . . who hath established in (their) courses the lights (of heaven) for determining seasons from year to year . . . . Since the generations of old they have not withdrawn from their path, unless God commanded them (so to do) by the command of His servants" (18:11-12; all extracts trans. G.B. Gray).

The Testament of Levi, part of the Testaments of the Twelve Patriarchs, a pseudepigraphic work by a Jewish author of the 2nd century B.C. but modeled on Jacob's final testament to his sons (Genesis 49), contains one of the most splendid messianic predictions of all. Inasmuch as Levi was the ancestor of Israel's hereditary sacerdotal tribe, the vision of the Messiah here is one of the ultimate High Priest: "And after their punishment shall have come from the Lord, the priesthood shall fail. Then shall the Lord raise up a new priest. And to him all the words of the Lord shall be revealed; And he shall execute a righteous judgment upon the earth for a multitude of days" (18:1-2). His coming will bring light and peace to the whole earth, and from heaven sanctification will come upon him in the Father's voice. "In his priesthood shall sin come to an end, and the lawless shall cease to do evil, [and the just shall rest in him]. And he shall open the gates of paradise, and shall remove the threatening sword against Adam. And he shall give to the saints to eat from the tree of life. . .And he shall give power to His children to tread upon the evil spirits. And the Lord shall rejoice in his children, and be well pleased in His beloved ones for ever" (18:9-10, 12-13; all extracts trans. R.H. Charles). Phrases from this text resound in early Christian liturgies. Compare the eucharistic Prayer of Hippolytus: "He carried out your will, acquiring for you a holy people by stretching out his hands as he suffered, to free from suffering those who believe in you. He was handed over in voluntary suffering, so as to destroy death and break the chains of the devil, trample hell underfoot, bring light to the just, establish the rule of faith and manifest the resurrection . . . ." And this folk prayer from Armenia: "The dawn grows white. I see the Cross shimmer again. My Lord is a sweet Lord. The gates reopen in Paradise, and those of hell are smashed to bits. My whole soul is freed; and Christ lifts me up in his arms."

E. *A Newly Ordered World:* *Isaiah 11:1-10; 65:17-25; 66:7-24.*
[*From the* Pseudepigrapha: *Apocalypse of Baruch (2 Baruch) 30:1 through 32:6; 47:1 through 48:24.* Charles, vol. II, pp. 498-499, 504-506; Charlesworth, Vol. One, pp. 631, 635-636; De Lange, pp. 220-222. *1 Enoch 1:3-10; 5:8-10; 39:4-7; 91:16-17.* Charles, Vol. II, pp. 188-190, 210-211, 265; Charlesworth, Vol. One, pp. 13-15, 31,73.]
The concept of a "new world" has been perennially appealing to believers resident in North America. Indeed, the phrase, *novus ordo seclorum,* "a new order of the ages," appears on the reverse of the Great Seal of the United States. Ralph Waldo Emerson, writing in the 1830s when the young republic was discovering its own character and moral perspective, felt compelled to say, "the knowledge of man is an evening knowledge,...but that of God is a morning knowledge...The problem of restoring to the world original and eternal beauty, is solved by the redemption of the soul. The ruin or the blank, that we see when we look at nature, is in our own eye. . .The reason why the world lacks unity, and lies broken and in heaps, is, because man is disunited with himself. . .There are innocent men who worship God after the tradition of their fathers, but their sense of duty has not yet extended to the use of all their faculties. . .But when a faithful thinker, resolute to detach every object from personal relations, and see it in the light of thought, shall, at the same time, kindle science with the fire of the holiest affections, then will God go forth anew into creation."

This appeal for a new vision and a new style of living, like others which have succeeded it in the public discourse of America (such as songs about an answer blowing in the wind, Black and White together, give peace a chance, and the dawn of the age of Aquarius — current in the 1960s), is derivative from the peaceable kingdom tradition of the Isaiah school of prophecy, whose hearers, at various crisis points in the history of Israel, longed for the corruption of the human sphere to be abolished, and the perfection of a world renewed by God's mercy to be established, much as believers yearn nowadays.

Isaiah 11:1-10 is the key text for all Judeo-Christian conceptions of a divinely re-ordered realm. Scholars variously regard it as a fragment of a Davidic enthronement liturgy or as an oracle envisaging the restoration of an interrupted Davidic monarchic lineage:

"There shall come forth a shoot from the stump of Jesse, and a branch shall grow out of his roots" (11:1). This awesome ruler is endowed by the Spirit of God with gifts of discernment that afford him insights not available by means of the fallible human senses and faculties, enabling him to dispatch the fallacious and derisive wicked with a mere breath: "Righteousness shall be the girdle of his waist, and faithfulness the girdle of his loins" (11:5).

Moreover, as Elmer A. Leslie notes, "in 11:6-9 there is lifted up a characteristic feature of the messianic hope which includes peace between animals and human beings and between men themselves. The climactic feature of this hope is that just as waters cover the deep, so knowledge of the Lord will fill the whole earth." The beatific vision is carried further in passages from the final segment of the Isaiah tradition that tell of newly-created heavens and earth (65:17-25) and a rejuvenated Jerusalem miraculously delivered of new offspring (66:7-24). "The characteristic of the Zion in this new universe is joy," notes the Jesuit scholar John L. McKenzie. "The children of the new Jerusalem are compared, somewhat broadly, to infants at the breast. The rare comparision of Yahweh to a mother illustrates not only his care but his tenderness."

The final oracle in the Isaiah tradition is that God will gather all nations, with those who have seen his glory being sent to the most distant coasts to bring all of Israel's kindred believers to Zion as a living offering to the Lord. The pseudepigraphic Apocalypse of Baruch, which may date from after the destruction of the Temple in A.D. 70, extends the ingathering even further: "Then all who have fallen asleep in hope of [the Messiah] shall rise again ... and they shall come forth, and a multitude of souls shall be seen together in one assemblage of one thought, and the first shall rejoice and the last shall not be grieved. For they know that the time has come of which it is said, that it is the consummation of the times" (30:1-3). Therefore faithful people should look beyond the present anguish of Jerusalem. "For there will be a greater trial ... when the Mighty one will renew His creation" (32:6).

The prophet's own response to the turmoil of his day and age is a wonderful declaration of confidence in God's benevolent will: "O my Lord, thou summonest the advent of the times, and they stand before

Thee; Thou causest the power of the ages to pass away, and they do not resist Thee. . .In Thee do we trust, for lo! Thy law is with us, and we know that we shall not fall so long as we keep Thy statutes. . .For we are all one celebrated people, who have received one law from One: And the law which is amongst us will aid us, and the surpassing wisdom which is in us will help us" (48:2,22,24; all extracts trans. R.H. Charles).

1 Enoch, also an apocalyptic work of Jewish origin, dates from the period of the 2nd century B.C. to the 1st century A.D. It had considerable influence on early Christian writers, most notably the author of the Letter of Jude, in which quotations from it appear. It purports to be the spiritual legacy of the primal ancestor Enoch, who, as Genesis 5:4 says, "walked with God; and he was not, for God took him." The eschatological predictions and visions made known in 1 Enoch are supposedly the result of Enoch's traversal of earth, hell and heaven during God's taking of him into his eternal presence. At the end of time, on "the day of tribulation," according to Enoch's vision, "the Holy Great One will come forth from His dwelling. . .And there shall be a judgment upon all. . .But with the righteous He will make peace, and will protect the elect, and mercy shall be upon them. . . . And then there shall be bestowed upon the elect wisdom, and they shall all live and never again sin, either through ungodliness or through pride: But they who are wise shall be humble. . .And their lives shall be increased in peace, and the years of their joy shall be multiplied, in eternal gladness and peace, all the days of their life" (1:1,3,8; 5:8-9).

Further on "in those days a whirlwind carried me off from the earth, and set me down at the end of the heavens. And there I saw another vision, the dwelling-places of the holy, and the resting-places of the righteous. . . . And in that place mine eyes saw the Elect One of righteousness and of faith, and I saw his dwelling-place under the wings of the Lord of Spirits. And righteousness shall prevail in his days, and the righteous and elect shall be without number before Him for ever and ever. And all the righteous and elect before Him shall be strong as fiery lights, and their mouth shall be full of blessing" (39:3-4,6-7).

Finally, he discerns that "the first heaven shall depart and pass away, and a new heaven shall appear, and all the powers of the heavens shall give sevenfold light. And after that there will be many weeks without number for ever, and all shall be in goodness and righteousness, and sin shall no more be mentioned for ever" (91:16-17; all extracts trans. R.H. Charles).

F. *The Consummation of the Times*: *The Prayer of Manasseh. The Prayer of Azaiah (Song of the Three Young Men) 3-20a.* [*From* The Dead Sea Scrolls: *Hymn Scroll III: 19-22.* Vermes, 3rd edn., pp. 172-173. *VII: 26-28.* Vermes, p. 186. *X: 3-14.* Vermes, pp. 192-193. *Community Rule (Manual of Discipline) X: 9-19.* Vermes, pp. 76-77. *XI: 15-17.* Vermes, p. 80.] It is an interesting and praiseworthy characteristic of the Israelite spirit that momentous junctures in the course of time are marked by the impulse to offer confession and make atonement. Indeed, the celebration of the beginning of the liturgical new year in Judaism, Rosh Hashanah, is closely followed by the Day of Atonement, Yom Kippur. And one of the first concerns of devout Jews after the final destruction of the Temple in A.D. 70 was to determine where and how they were to bring before God the atonement which the Torah required and their hearts yearned to pour fort

In the two centuries preceding that horrendous event, Jewish spiritual literature teemed with prayers of expiation. One of the most beautiful is that which is entitled the Prayer of Manasseh, inspired by the claim of 2 Chronicles 33:11-13 that this appalling son of King Hezekiah repented of his sins of idolatry and ritual infanticide during a brief period of exile. The prayer opens with a glorious encomium of the Creator: "Almighty Lord, God of our fathers, of Abraham, Isaac, and Jacob, and of their righteous posterity, who made heaven and earth in their manifold array...The majesty of your glory is more than can be borne; none can endure the threat of your wrath against sinners" (vv. 1-2,5; REB). God's mercy is then praised and invoked, and the prayer concludes where it began, with an ascription of glory which unites God's servants on earth and in heaven: "I shall praise you continually all the days of my life. The whole host of heaven sings your praise, and yours is the glory for ever" (v. 15; REB).

It behooved the righteous no less than the wicked to offer prayers of confession. One such is the prayer of Azariah, which was inserted into the Greek version of the Book of Daniel: "Blessed are you and worthy of praise, Lord, the God of our fathers; your name is glorious for ever: you are just in all you have done to us; all your works are true; your paths are straight, your judgments all true." This acknowledgement is no vapid generalization: "Just is the sentence in all that you have brought on us and on Jerusalem, the holy city of our ancestors; true and just the sentence you have passed upon our sins" (vv. 3-5). Hardest of all confessions to make is one in which the rightness of God's actions is extolled even when punishment is visited upon the innocent members of God's people (like Azariah) as well as the guilty. The sanctity of the community of faith is only as strong as that of its weakest members.

Such was certainly the perspective of the Jewish religious fellowship responsible for the compiling and secreting of the Dead Sea Scrolls. "The Qumran community," writes Millar Burrows, the scholar of biblical theology who was so instrumental in making known the scrolls' importance, "was convinced that it was in sight of the continental divide of history." Not only, therefore, did these sectarians—usually identified as Essenes—who lived an ascetic life by the shores of the Dead Sea, transcribe for their own diligent study the texts of the Hebrew Scriptures, but they made commentaries on them and used them as models for hymns of their own composing which they chanted in their communal worship.

This liturgical poetry has an eerie but compelling beauty, and it exemplifies the eschatological mood prevalent in the Holy Land in the centuries immediately before and after the birth of Jesus of Nazareth. "The spirit of the times, both within and without the community of Qumran, was that of apocalyptic waiting and legalistic observance of the commandments in preparation for the coming struggle and deliverance. The whole situation—political, social, and spiritual—had changed from one of national pride and prosperity, economic and political corruption, and spiritual complacency to one of national humiliation, foreign domination, disillusionment and fear. It was the kind of situation that always favors a resort to apocalyptic dreams."

One of the Qumran hymns begins with an encomium addressed to God: "I thank Thee, O Lord, for thou hast redeemed my soul from the

Pit. . .I walk on limitless level ground, and I know there is hope for him whom thou hast shaped from dust. . .Thou hast allotted to man an everlasting destiny. . .that he may praise Thy Name in a common rejoicing and recount Thy marvels before all Thy works" (III:19-22).

According to their own writings, the community was founded by a leader whom they called the "teacher of righteousness," a devout man who vehemently rejected the priestly and royal establishment of Judea in the 1st century B.C. and imparted to his followers his own special insights into God's unwavering truth. Another of their hymns reflects the founder's teachings: "I [thank Thee, O Lord], for Thou hast enlightened me through Thy truth. . .Who is like Thee among the gods, O Lord, and who is according to Thy truth? Who, when he is judged, shall be righteous before Thee?" (VII:26-28).

Yet another hymn sharply contrasts the completeness and perfection that is God and the nonentity that is the human creature: "What then is man that is earth, that is shaped [from clay] and returns to the dust, that Thou shouldst give him to understand such marvels and make known to him the counsel of [Thy truth]?. . . Beside Thee there is nothing, and nothing can compare with Thee in strength; in the presence of Thy glory there is nothing, and Thy might is without price. Who among Thy great and marvelous creatures can stand in the presence of Thy glory? How then can he who returns to his dust? For Thy glory's sake alone hast Thou made all these things" (X:3-14, excerpted).

Much of the community's doctrine is embodied in a document known variously to scholars as The Community Rule or The Manual of Discipline. It contains the sect's rules of conduct and the various precepts which governed all its undertakings. Appended to it are some stanzas to be used when an initiate is received into the community. Here are some noteworthy extracts: "I will sing with knowledge and all my music shall be for the glory of God . . . and when evening and morning depart I will recite His decrees. . .I will say to God, 'My Righteousness; and 'Author of my Goodness' to the Most High, 'Fountain of Knowledge' and 'Source of Holiness,' 'Summit of Glory' and 'Almighty Eternal Majesty.' I will choose that which He teaches me and will delight in His judgment of me. . .I will bless Him for His exceeding wonderful deeds at the beginning of fear and dread

139

and in the abode of distress and desolation. . .I know that judgment of all the living is in His hand, and that all His deeds are truth. I will praise Him when distress is unleashed and will magnify Him also because of his salvation" (X:9-19,excerpted).

Benedictions are characteristic of Jewish prayer; here is one used at Qumran: "Blessed art thou, my God, who openest the heart of thy servant to knowledge!. . .without Thee no way is perfect, and without Thy will nothing is done. It is Thou who hast taught all knowledge and all things come to pass by Thy will" (XI:15-17; all extracts trans. Geza Vermes).

If any part of an archaeological site is cause for what the Roman poet Vergil called *lacrimae rerum*, "tears over the way things are," the pottery dump is it. Here the excavators have discarded the less significant shards they have unearthed of water jars, cooking utensils, tableware, lamps and other bits of fired clay—remains of the very objects that remind people now alive that their predecessors had the same daily needs as themselves: to keep clean, feed themselves and light their rooms at night. The detritus of broken pots at Qumran is immense, which is all the more shocking because the religious community there was abstemious and wasted little. Roman legionaries making a strategic sweep or Jewish partisans on a raid did most of the damage, no doubt overcome by one of those moods of frustration and rage that seem to be an inevitable element of soldiering. What little the warriors left intact, wandering Bedouin herdspeople totaled. How many dwelling-places of God-fearing men and women have been left like this, shattered and desolate, over the course of time? How many are yet to experience such wastage? Happily, the story of faith in the one eternal God did not come to an end in a rubbish heap beside the Dead Sea

Not far from Qumran, while its religious community still flourished, a carpenter from Nazareth underwent baptism in the river Jordan, experienced the Spirit of God descending upon him, and began to share with people from far and near the good news of God's reign. And six centuries later, a merchant from Mecca was called to recite to all who would listen the truth of God, the merciful and compassionate. Year upon year, moreover, the sons and daughters of

Israel, though devastated by the destruction of the Temple on Mount Zion, and scattered across the face of the earth, have painstakingly borne witness to God's gracious will through their recitation of the Torah and their performance of acts of mercy. How shameful, therefore, that the adepts of these three parallel and complementary developments of faith have all too seldom cooperated in bringing succor and salvation to humankind, but instead have squandered their God-given resources and energies in disputing—sometimes, indeed, persecuting and destroying—one another. May God forgive us.

On King David Street in modern Jerusalem, not too distant from where the Dead Sea Scrolls are now displayed, stands the study center of Hebrew Union College, the theological school of Reform Judaism. Its chapel is a rarity in a city that is overburdened with the trappings and gewgaws of religiosity: a plain, honest house of worship, a place where one may be still, and know that God is God (Psalm 46:11). I first visited it with my mother and father in the mid-1960s when I was a college student. We were shown the chapel by none other than Hebrew Union's president of blessed memory, Dr. Nelson Glueck, my parents' fellow-scholar and friend over many years. I had been aware of him by reputation and through his writings as an outstanding archaeologist. In the flesh, he revealed himself as a person of extraordinary though unconventional spiritual qualities; his eyes blazed with the inner light of one who had gone into the desert and had been accosted there by the Divine. What he showed us was unforgettable. The chapel's focus was two massive slabs of blood-purple polished stone which dominated an entire wall. They served as doors to the Ark holding the Torah scrolls. "Go on, open them," Rabbi Glueck invited us. We hesitated, perhaps because there was no apparent handhold. "Here, let me show you," he offered, and with one finger he swung open the ponderous but perfectly balanced doors. "See," he said. "This is what we want everyone to realize about the Word of God: that it is awesome, solid, enduring forever—yet it can be opened with the gentlest touch."

Go on, open the scriptures.

Sources of Quotations

Preface

The Analects of Confucius. Translated from the Chinese, with an Introduction and
        Notes, by Lionel Giles. Norwalk, CT: The Heritage Press, 1970; p. 26.

Thomas Jefferson: "A Bill for Establishing Religious Freedom" (1777, 1779), quoted
        from *Writings,* ed. Merrill D. Peterson. New York: The Library of America,
        1984; p. 346.

Elias Bickerman: *Four Strange Books of the Bible*. New York: Schocken Books, 1967;
        p. 9.

"Lord of heaven and earth" in Giovanni Pettinato: *The Archives of Ebla: An Empire
        Inscribed in Clay*. Garden City, NY: Doubleday & Company, Inc., 1981;
        p. 259.

"The Hymn to the Aton," translated by John A. Wilson, in James B. Pritchard, ed.: *The
        Ancient Near East: An Anthology of Texts and Pictures*. Princeton, NJ: Prin-
        ceton University Press, 1958; p. 229. (Hereafter cited as *ANET&P.*)

Jorg Zink's edition of the Hebrew Scriptures, which prompted the present reading plan,
        is *Das Alte Testament* ausgewahlt, ubertragen und in geschichtlicher Folge
        angeordnet von Jorg Zink. Stuttgart and Berlin: Kreuz-Verlag, 1966.

Wayfaring Strangers

Anthony Hecht quotation and words from the Passover liturgy are cited from *A Passover
        Haggadah:* The New Union Haggadah Edited by Herbert Bronstein for the
        Central Conference of American Rabbis. New York: Grossman Publishers,
        A Division of The Viking Press, 1974, rpt. Penguin Books, 1978; pp. 17, 29,
        45.

Julian Morgenstern: *The Book of Genesis: A Jewish Interpretation*. Second Edition. New
        York: Schocken Books, 1965; pp. 98-99, 253-255.

E. A. Speiser: *Genesis*.   The Anchor Bible. Garden City, NY: Doubleday & Company,
        Inc., 1964; p. 182.

Al-Qur'an. A Contemporary Translation by Ahmed Ali. Princeton, NJ: Princeton
        University Press, 1988; p. 200.

Israel's Wilderness Encounter with God

Henry David Thoreau quotations from the essay "Walking" and from *A Week on the
        Concord and Merrimack Rivers.*

Quotations from the Passover liturgy are cited from *A Passover Haggadah*, as above,
        pp. 26, 48-49.

Everett Fox: *Now These Are the Names*. A New English Rendering of the Book of
        Exodus. New York: Schocken Books, 1986; pp. 7-8.

Theodor H. Gaster: *Festivals of the Jewish Year: A Modern Interpretation and Guide*.

New York: William Sloane Associates, 1953, rpt. William Morrow and Company, Inc., 1971; p. 32.

Sir Thomas Browne quotation from *Religio Medici.*

Abraham Joshua Heschel: *God in Search of Man: A Philosophy of Judaism.* Philadelphia: The Jewish Publication Society of America, 1955, rpt .New York: Farrar, Straus and Giroux Inc., 1976; p. 138.

Philip Potter: "Together Seeking God's Face," in *The Ecumenical Review*, Vol. XXVIII No. 2, April 1976; pp. 206-207.

Bound for the Promised Land

G. Ernest Wright in *Joshua.* A New Translation with Notes and Commentary by Robert G. Boling, Introduction by G. Ernest Wright. The Anchor Bible. Garden City, NY: Doubleday & Company, Inc., 1982; pp. 5-6.

Max Apple in David Rosenberg, ed.: *Congregation: Contemporary Writers Read the Jewish Bible.* San Diego, etc.: Harcourt Brace Jovanovich, 1987; pp. 65, 67-68.

Twelve Tribes, One Nation.

Lawrence E. Toombs: "The Psalms" in Charles M. Laymon, ed.: *The Interpreter's One-Volume Commentary on the Bible.* Nashville, etc.: Abingdon Press, 1971; p. 281.

Robert G. Boling: *Judges.* The Anchor Bible. Garden City, NY: Doubleday & Company, Inc., 1975; p. 4.

Crowning Achievement of Nationhood

Walter Brueggemann: *David's Truth in Israel's Imagination & Memory.* Philadelphia: Fortress Press, 1985; p. 13.

Bertolt Brecht: *Die Dreigroschenoper.* Berlin: Suhrkamp Verlag, 1955, rpt. 1962; p. 92. Translated by D.E.J.

Thomas Merton: *Praying the Psalms.* Collegeville, MN: The Liturgical Press, 1956. p.3.

Albert Einstein: *Mein Weltbild.* Frankfurt am Main: Ullstein Bucher, 1970; pp. 9-10. English version in *Living Philosophies* (New York: Simon and Schuster, 1931; pp. 6-7) slightly adapted in conformity with the original German text.

Charles L. Taylor: *Let the Psalms Speak.* Greenwich, CT: The Seabury Press, 1961; pp. 48-49.

Edward F. Campbell, Jr.: *Ruth.* The Anchor Bible. Second Edition. Garden City, NY: Doubleday & Company, Inc. 1975; pp. 10, 28.

Thomas Traherne quotation from *Centuries of Meditations.*

"The Instruction of Amen-em-Opet," translated by John A. Wilson, in James B. Pritchard, ed.: *ANET&P*, as above, p. 238.

A House Divided Against Itself

Edith Hamilton: *Spokesmen for God*. New York: W.W. Norton & Company, Inc., 1949; pp. 70, 82-83.

Bernhard W. Anderson: *Understanding the Old Testament*. Fourth Edition. Englewood Cliffs, NJ: Prentice-Hall, 1986; pp. 260-261.

Davie Napier: *Song of the Vineyard: A Guide through the Old Testament*. Revised Edition. Philadelphia: Fortress Press, 1981; p. 147.

Davie Napier: *Word of God, Word of Earth*. Philadelphia: Pilgrim Press, 1976; p. 67.

Mary Ellen Chase: *The Prophets for the Common Reader*. New York: W.W. Norton & Company, Inc. 1963; pp. 80-81.

James Atlas in David Rosenberg, ed.: *Congregation*, as above; p. 194.

J.B. Phillips: *Four Prophets*. New York: The Macmillan Company, 1963; pp. 59-60.

Judah after Israel's Downfall.

The Oriental Institute Prism of Sennacherib, translated by A. Leo Oppenheim, in James B. Pritchard, ed.: *ANET&P*, p. 200.

Marianne Micks in *Proclamation 3: Epiphany*. Series A. Aids for Interpreting the Church Year. Philadelphia: Fortress Press, 1986; p. 32.

Abraham J. Heschel: *The Prophets*. Volume I. New York: Harper & Row, 1969; p. 18.

W. Gunther Plaut, *et al.: The Torah: A Modern Commentary*. New York: Union of American Hebrew Congregations, 1981; pp. 1293, 1296.

Dietrich Bonhoeffer: *Letters and Papers from Prison*. The Enlarged Edition. New York: The Macmillan Company, 1972; p. 74.

Stephen Berg in David Rosenberg, ed.: *Congregation*, as above; pp. 239-240.

Dietrich Bonhoeffer: *Psalms: The Prayer Book of the Bible*. Minneapolis: Augsburg Publishing House, 1970; p. 41.

Judah Brought Very Low

Moshe Greenberg: *Ezekiel 1-20*. The Anchor Bible. Garden City, NY: Doubleday & Company, Inc., 1983; p. 187.

Sheldon H. Blank: *Jeremiah: Man and Prophet*. Cincinnati: Hebrew Union College Press, 1961; pp. 227, 230-231.

By the Waters of Babylon

John Hollander in David Rosenberg, ed.: *Congregation*, as above; p. 308.

Daniel Berrigan: *Uncommon Prayer*. A Crossroad Book. New York: The Seabury Press, 1978; pp. 62-63, 66.

Abraham Joshua Heschel: *God in Search of Man*, as above; pp. 378-379.

That He May Raise, the Lord Throws Down

Cyrus Cylinder, translated by A. Leo Oppenheim, in James B. Pritchard, ed.: *ANET&P*, as above; pp. 206-207.

James Luther Mays: *Ezekiel, Second Isaiah*. Proclamation Commentaries. Philadelphia: Fortress Press, 1978; p. 46.

Dietrich Bonhoeffer: *Creation and Fall*. New York: The Macmillan Company, 1959; p. 22.

Martin Buber: *The Prophetic Faith*. New York: The Macmillan Company, 1949, rpt. New York: Harper and Brothers, 1960; pp. 206, 222-223.

Pierre Teilhard de Chardin: *The Divine Milieu*. New York: Harper & Row, 1960; pp. 59-61.

The Fortunes of Zion Restored

Cyrus Cylinder, translated by A. Leo Oppenheim, in James B. Pritchard, ed.: *ANET&P*, as above; p. 208.

Elmer A. Leslie: *The Psalms*. Nashville, etc.: Abingdon Press, 1949; p. 128.

Jay Neugeboren in David Rosenberg, ed.: *Congregation*, as above; p. 460.

Ernest Payne in David M. Paton, ed.: *Breaking Barriers: Nairobi 1975*. The Official Report of the Fifth Assembly of the World Council of Churches. Grand Rapids: Wm. B. Eerdmans, 1976; p. 270.

John L. McKenzie, S.J.: *Second Isaiah*. The Anchor Bible. Garden City, NY: Doubleday & Company, Inc., 1968; pp. 1xviii-1xix.

Davie Napier: *Song of the Vineyard*, as above; p. 270.

In the House Not Made with Hands

H.R.H. the Prince of Wales quoted in *The New York Times*, October 30, 1988.

Forest Whitaker quoted in *Esquire,* December 1988; p. 118.

Stephen Mitchell: *The Book of Job*. San Francisco: North Point Press, 1987; pp. xv-xvi, 79, 88.

Leopoldo Niilus: unattributed contribution in David Enderton Johnson, ed.: *Uppsala to Nairobi,* 1968-1975, Report of the Central Committee to the Fifth Assembly of the World Council of Churches. New York: Friendship Press, 1975; pp. 136-137.

Dietrich Bonhoeffer: *Letters and Papers from Prison*, as above; p. 400.

Mitchell Dahood, S.J.: *Psalms III, 101-150*. The Anchor Bible. Garden City, NY: Doubleday & Company, Inc., 1970; p. 155.

Harvey H. Guthrie, Jr.: *Israel's Sacred Songs: A Study of Dominant Themes*. New York: The Seabury Press, 1966; p. 149.

My Thoughts Were Steady

Charles L. Taylor: *Layman's Guide to 70 Psalms*. Nashville, etc.: Abingdon Press, 1973;
    p. 8.

Ronald Knox: *The Psalms: A New Translation.* New York: Sheed & Ward, 1955; p. 174.

Nicholas de Lange: *Apocrypha: Jewish Literature of the Hellenistic Age*. New York: The
    Viking Press, 1978: p. 179.

David Winston: *The Wisdom of Solomon*. The Anchor Bible. Garden City, NY: Dou-
    bleday & Company, Inc., 1979; p. 112.

Robert Gordis: *The Book of God and Man: A Study of Job*. Chicago, etc.:The University
    of Chicago Press, 1965; p. 278.

Elmer A. Leslie: *The Psalms*, as above; pp. 414-415, 409.

Charles L. Taylor: *Layman's Guide to 70 Psalms*, as above; p. 52.

Mitchell Dahood, S.J.: *Psalms III, 101-150*, as above; p. 227.

God's Kingdom Tarries Long

Martin Buber: *The Way of Response*. Selections from His Writings Edited by N.N.
    Glatzer. New York: Schocken Books, 1966; p. 186.

Bertolt Brecht: *Die Dreigroschenoper*, as above; p. 49. Translated by D.E.J.

Martin Buber: "The Demand of the Spirit and Historical Reality" in *Pointing the Way:
    Collected Essays.* New York: Harper and Brothers, 1957; pp. 188-189.

Mitchell Dahood, S.J.: *Psalms II, 51-100*. Garden City, N.Y: Doubleday & Company,
    Inc., 1968; p. 370.

Martin Buber: "Gandhi, Politics, and Us" in *Pointing the Way,* as above; p. 131.

Alexander A. Di Lella in *The Book of Daniel*. A New Translation with Notes and
    Commentary on Chapters 1-9 by Louis F. Hartman, C.SS.R. Introduction,
    and Commentary on Chapters 10-12 by Alexander A. Di Lella, O.F.M. The
    Anchor Bible. Garden City, NY: Doubleday & Company, Inc., 1978; p. 107.

Peter R. Ackroyd in Charles M. Laymon, ed.: *The Interpreter's One-Volume Commen-
    tary on the Bible,* as above; p. 345.

John Bright: *Jeremiah*. The Anchor Bible. Garden City, NY: Doubleday & Company,
    Inc., 1965; p. 119.

Sheldon H. Blank: *Jeremiah: Man and Prophet,* as above; p. 124.

Carey A. Moore: *Daniel, Esther and Jeremiah: The Additions*. The Anchor Bible.
    Garden City, NY: Doubleday & Company, Inc., 1977; p. 313.

Joseph Klausner: *The Messianic Idea in Israel.* New York: The Macmillan Company,
    1955; p. 138.

Francine Prose in David Rosenberg, ed.: *Congregation*, as above; p. 281.

Ralph Waldo Emerson quotation from *Nature*, Chapter VIII: Prospects.

Elmer A. Leslie: *Isaiah*. New York, etc.: Abingdon Press, 1963; p. 63.

John L. McKenzie, S.J.: *Second Isaiah*, as above; pp. 200, 209.

Millar Burrows: "Prophecy and the Prophets at Qumran" in Bernhard W. Anderson and

Walter Harrelson, eds.: *Israel's Prophetic Heritage*. New York: Harper &
        Brothers, 1962; pp. 230, 226.
G. Vermes: *The Dead Sea Scrolls in English*. Third Edition. London, New York, etc.:
        Penguin Books, 1987; pp. 212-213, 172-173, 186, 192-193, 76-77, 80.

Quotations from the Bible are from the following translations:
Unless otherwise noted, scripture quotations are from the Revised Standard Version of
the Bible, Copyright 1946, 1952, © 1971, 1973, and from the Apocrypha, Copyright
© 1957, by the Division of Christian Education of the National Council of Churches of
Christ in the U.S.A., and are used by permission .

Scripture quotations identified (GNB) are from the *Good News Bible with Deuteroca-
        nonicals/Apocrypha* in Today's English Version. Copyright © American
        Bible Society 1966, 1971, 1976, 1979.
Scripture passages marked (KJV) are from the Authorized or King James Version, first
        published in 1611.
Scripture selections marked (NAB) are taken from the New American Bible, Copyright
        1970 by the Confraternity of Christian Doctrine, Washington, D.C. and are
        used with permission. All rights reserved.
Scripture quotations marked (NEB) are from the New English Bible. Copyright © the
        Delegates of the Oxford University Press and the Syndics of the Cambridge
        University Press, 1961, 1970. Reprinted by permission.
Scripture quotations marked (NJB) are from the New Jerusalem Bible. Copyright © 1985
        by Darton, Longman & Todd, Ltd. and Doubleday & Company, Inc. Per-
        mission granted by DOUBLEDAY a division of Bantam, Doubleday, Dell
        Publishing Group, Inc.
Scripture quotations marked (REB) are from The Revised English Bible with the Apo-
        crypha. © Oxford University Press and Cambridge University Press 1989.
        Reprinted by permission.
Quotations from the Psalms marked (BCP) are taken from the Psalter of *The Book of
        Common Prayer* According to the use of The Episcopal Church. © Copy-
        right 1977 by Charles Mortimer Guilbert as Custodian of the Standard Book
        of Common Prayer. All rights reserved.

Resources For Studying The Hebrew Scriptures

Listed here with brief descriptive comments are a few books on the Hebrew Scriptures and related writings which adult lay people may find useful as they pursue their study of God's Word. (For general works on the Bible, see the bibliography in my *Opening the New Testament,* also published by Forward Movement.) I have made a special point of noting worthwhile and ecumenically-aware works of reputable scholarship by both Jewish and Christian authors whose intended readership is primarily the general public, not fellow specialists. While it is true that today, as in the past, Christianity and Judaism tend to read the sacred texts of ancient Israel from different dogmatic and experiential points of view, members of either faith—and persons adherent to neither—can learn much through examining what scrupulous and well-informed commentators from both traditions have to say about the writings held in equal esteem by all people of the Book. Rest assured that while words of scripture may be printed in Hebrew characters in one or two of the books recommended here, such passages are always fully translated into English also, and no knowledge is expected of any reader beyond what he or she is likely to have acquired in a normal college education.

Introductions to the Hebrew Scriptures

Bernhard W. Anderson: *Understanding the Old Testament.* Fourth Edition. Englewood Cliffs, NJ: Prentice-Hall, 1986; 685 pp. (A clearly-written and aptly-illustrated introduction to the Old Testament as the faith record of ancient Israel, it lucidly describes the relationship of the Hebrew Scriptures to archaeological data and other historical evidence.)

Lawrence Boadt: *Reading the Old Testament: An Introduction.* New York, etc.: Paulist Press, 1984; 569 pp. (A worthwhile approach, especially for those interested in how the Old Testament relates to the whole cultural realm of the ancient Near East.)

Davie Napier: *Song of the Vineyard: A Guide through the Old Testament.* Revised Edition. Philadelphia: Fortress Press, 1981; 335 pp. (Focusing largely on the Hebrew Scriptures as story and poetry, this is a very insightful reading companion by a gifted theologian and poet.)

Jon D. Levenson: *Sinai and Zion: An Entry into the Jewish Bible.* San Francisco: Harper & Row, 1985; 227 pp. (This brief but excellent book by a leading Hebrew scholar not only draws attention to the major themes of the Hebrew Scriptures but connects them with the teachings of later rabbinic tradition and the theological insights of the synagogue liturgy.)

Bruce C. Birch: *What Does the Lord Require? The Old Testament Call to Social Witness.* Philadelphia: The Westminster Press, 1985; 119 pp. (The Hebrew Scriptures are anything but an abstract theological treatise; they are the expression of faith in action. In a clear and lively fashion, Dr. Birch demonstrates the ways in which Israel's Torah and prophets are the foundation for the imperative of social justice in Christianity.)

The Torah

W. Gunther Plaut, *et al.: The Torah: A Modern Commentary.* New York: Union of American Hebrew Congregations, 1981; 1787 pp. (An authoritative but eminently readable commentary produced under Reform Jewish auspices, it includes lucid introductions, summary comments, footnotes and "gleanings"—notable observations from later Jewish tradition or by renowned Jewish and Christian authors.)

Thomas W. Mann: *The Book of the Torah.* Atlanta: John Knox Press, 1988; 180 pp. (Scholars have tended to study the Pentateuch by separating out the various sources underlying the received text of the Torah. In his very helpful book, Dr. Mann, a United Church of Christ scholar, gives an integrative interpretation, emphasizing the literary and theological coherence of the Torah's major units.)

The Historical Books.

Walter E. Rast: *Joshua, Judges, Samuel, Kings.* Proclamation Commentaries. Philadelphia: Fortress Press, 1978; 124 pp. (The major historical books are no mere chronology of events, but an interpretation of such events according to a distinct theological viewpoint, which Dr. Rast, a Lutheran theologian, examines, high-lighting several key concepts, such as covenant, law and grace, Temple and kingship.)

Walter Brueggemann: *David's Truth in Israel's Imagination & Memory.* Philadelphia: Fortress Press, 1985; 128 pp. (A lively examination of four different narratives concerning the fascinating man who was Israel's greatest king.)

Davie Napier: *Word of God, Word of Earth.* Philadelphia: Pilgrim Press, 1976; 105 pp. (A wide-ranging, thought-provoking study of the account in 1 Kings 17-21 of the deeds of Elijah, Israel's pre-eminent prophet.)

Elias Bickerman: *From Ezra to the Last of the Maccabees.* New York: Schocken Books, 1962; 186 pp. (A brief, easy-to-follow account of the history of the Jewish people after their return from exile in Babylon; by a foremost expert on the period.)

The Prophets

John W. Miller: *Meet the Prophets: A beginner's guide to the books of the biblical prophets—their meaning then and now.* New York, etc.: Paulist Press, 1987; 250 pp. (The subtitle tells it all: brief accounts of each Hebrew prophet, his message, and its relevance; by a Christian lay teacher of religion.)

Edith Hamilton: *Spokesmen for God: The Great Teachers of the Old Testament.* New York: W.W. Norton & Company, Inc., 1949; 259 pp. (The great classical scholar's unsurpassed account of how the Hebrew prophets both reflected and outdistanced the intellectual and spiritual currents of the civilizations surrounding them.)

Abraham J. Heschel: *The Prophets.* New York: Harper & Row. Volume I, 1969; 235 pp. Volume II, 1971; 287 pp.(A profound yet very accessible study of the prophets and the major thrusts of their prophecy by the outstanding American Jewish theologian of this century.)

James M. Ward: *The Prophets*. Interpreting Biblical Texts. Nashville: Abingdon, 1982; 159 pp. (Dr. Ward, a United Methodist scholar, helps readers learn to interpret the prophets' messages by examining several key passages through a variety of means, including a comparison of several widely-used modern translations.)

The Psalms, Wisdom Literature and Other Writings

Roland E. Murphy, O.Carm.: *Wisdom Literature & Psalms*. Interpreting Biblical Texts. Nashville: Abingdon Press, 1983; 158 pp. (A fine overall sampling of this scriptural material by the noted Roman Catholic scholar.)

Gary Chamberlain, trans: *The Psalms: A New Translation for Prayer and Worship*. Nashville: The Upper Room, 1984; 187 pp. Peter Levi, trans.: *The Psalms*. With an introduction by Nicholas de Lange. Harmondsworth, etc.: Penguin Books, 1976; 239 pp. Francis Patrick Sullivan, trans.: *Lyric Psalms: Half a Psalter*. Washington, DC: The Pastoral Press, 1983; 192 pp. *Tragic Psalms*. Washington, DC: The Pastoral Press, 1987; 226 pp. (Sometimes new translations are what is necessary to induce new insights, and these three versions are in very different ways real eye- and ear-openers, as are the unconventional essays and reflections that accompany them.)

Mark S. Smith: *Psalms: The Divine Journey*. New York, etc.: Paulist Press, 1987; 85 pp. (This short book by a young Roman Catholic lay scholar is nothing short of brilliant; no matter how well you know the Psalms already, you'll experience them afresh if you read this book.)

C.S. Lewis: *Reflections on the Psalms*. New York: Harcourt, Brace and Company, 1958; 151 pp. (A perennial favorite by the Oxford scholar of English literature and Anglican lay theologian.)

Stephen Mitchell, trans.: *The Book of Job*. San Francisco: North Point Press, 1987; 129 pp. (A highly acclaimed translation of the Book of Job by a widely read scholar-poet-translator, with an insightful introductory essay.)

Nahum N. Glatzer, ed.: *The Dimensions of Job: A Study and Selected Readings*. New York: Schocken Books, 1969; 310 pp. (A wide-ranging sampling of reflections on Job by eminent writers of the Jewish, Christian and humanist traditions, including Buber, Kierkegaard, Renan, Chesterton, Gilbert Murray and James B. Conant.)

Marcia Falk, trans.: *The Song of Songs: Love Poems from the Bible*. New York, etc.: Harcourt Brace Jovanovich, 1977; 64 pp. (A magnificent poetic translation. *Note*: Dr. Falk's version has been republished in England with a fuller explanatory essay as *Love Lyrics from the Bible*. Sheffield: The Almond Press, 1982.)

Elias Bickerman: *Four Strange Books of the Bible*. New York: Schocken Books, 1967; 240 pp. (Lively, informative discussions of the Books of Jonah, Daniel, Ecclesiastes and Esther by a Jewish expert in the period when they were most likely written; Bickerman illuminates these works by apt quotations from the literature of surrounding cultures and citations from rabbinic and early Christian commentators.)

Editions and Commentaries on Ancient Hebrew and Near Eastern Texts outside the Jewish Scriptural Canon

Nicholas de Lange, ed. and trans.: *Apocrypha: Jewish Literature of the Hellenistic Age.* New York: The Viking Press, 1978; 244 pp. (An attractive, representative selection from the Apocrypha, Pseudepigrapha and Dead Sea Scrolls, with a helpful introduction, by the brilliant British rabbinic scholar.)

R.H. Charles, ed. and trans.: *The Apocrypha and Pseudepigrapha of the Old Testament.* Volume II, Pseudepigrapha. Oxford: at the Clarendon Press, 1913; 871 pp. (The pioneering edition in English of this important literature, it remains the most widely known.)

James H. Charlesworth, ed.: *The Old Testament Pseudepigrapha.* Garden City, NY: Doubleday & Company. Volume 1, 1983; 1056 pp. Volume 2, 1985; 1056 pp. (An exhaustively complete and scholarly yet quite readable edition, with a translation in the style of the Jerusalem Bible.)

Margaret Baker: *The Lost Prophet: The Book of Enoch and its influence on Christianity.* Nashville: Abingdon Press, 1989; 116 pp. (A fascinating and accessible study of the Jewish apocalyptic book quoted in the Letter of Jude and other early Christian writings.)

G. Vermes, ed. and trans.: *The Dead Sea Scrolls in English.* Third Edition. London, etc.: Penguin Books, 1987; 320 pp. (The fullest and most widely circulated translation of the Qumran texts.)

James B. Pritchard, ed.: *The Ancient Near East: An Anthology of Texts and Pictures.* Princeton, NJ: Princeton University Press, 1958; 380 pp. (Makes available for general readers the most important writings and inscriptions from the civilizations adjacent to ancient Israel.)

Also from Forward Movement

Opening the New Testament, by David E. Johnson.
Companion to *Opening the Hebrew Scriptures*.

The Daily Lectionary, by Joseph P. Russell. A four-book series giving a weekly overview and commentary for Bible readers using the daily office lectionary of the prayer book.

A Fresh Look at the Gospels, by Mary C. Morrison.
Designed to help readers look at the Bible as if they had never seen it before.

The Bible in the Household of Faith, by Geddes MacGregor. Fascinating insights in an examination of the Bible as literature.